My Whisper From God

MY WHISPER FROM GOD

Rachelle Law

MY WHISPER FROM GOD

A Heartfelt Testimony of Hope, Strength and Triumphs

By Rachelle Law

Rachelle Law

¹Children obey your parents in the Lord, for this is right.
² "Honour your father and mother" – which is the first
commandment with a promise – ³ "so that it may go well
with you and that you may enjoy long life on the earth."
Ephesians 6:1-3
New International Version (NIV)

Ernestine Marion Gilbert
(January 11, 1943–November 19, 2012)

Sylvester Mercer
(March 29, 1942–April 26, 2012)

Rachelle Law

ACKNOWLEDGEMENTS

There are simply not enough words or ways to say thank you to my mother, Ernestine Marion Gilbert. Thanks for loving me when I didn't love myself. You were the first to recognize the potential that was within me. Thanks Momma for everything. I AM what I AM because of my mom and the great I AM! Thanks for all you have given me and all you have given up for me. I am so thankful God chose you to be the chosen vessel to birth me into existence. Truth be told you are the true writer of the family. You showed me strength and perseverance to the very end.

To my only son Clarence Willard Smith Jr., there would be no story without you. I am forever grateful for the male role models; George Byers, Billy Williams, Sr. and Naleathon Byers who willingly gave of their time and of themselves to teach you the lessons I couldn't. You once said I was afraid of success. Well I no longer have that fear. Thank you son.

To my biggest supporters my beautiful daughters Michele and Ashley thanks for your unconditional love. It has been a long road; a journey of mountain highs and valley lows. There were times we were without money to pay bills and to buy food, yet you never complained or gave up on me. You taught me motherhood is like the two sides of a coin: there were days when I felt I was the head and I was on top of the world. Then there were days I felt like the tail. You encouraged me to hold on when everything around us was falling apart. There is no doubt that without your love, support, and constant encouragement this book would not be possible. Thanks for believing in me. I give you a standing ovation.

To Virginia Alder a key player, I appreciate your capable assistance in editing and proofreading. I am grateful to my son from another mother; Terrence Roland for his artistic skill with the cover design.

Thanks Christi for guiding me to a polished product with your professional editing skills. You have gone above and beyond the call of duty. Thank you for your honesty, encouragement, teaching and technical assistance.

I don't have enough space or ink to thank everybody so I will give a shout out to my husband, siblings, family and friends for your prayers and supporting me.

FOREWORD

In the Bible is recorded the story of a man named Job. God called Job more righteous than all who lived during that time. God allowed satan to put Job through a living hell and God never explained why. Can we trust a God who allows unspeakable pain in our lives with no explanation? Will we trust Him even then? In our pain, trauma and tragedy, is He still God?

What do we do with pain, loss, disappointment & death? As life happens, we're all certain to face each of these along the way. Some navigate these storms & valleys well. Others, not so much. For some, these challenges lead to an increasingly weary, worn & worried outlook on life. For other life travelers, these battles create courage, build boldness & forge faith.

Rachelle.

If you know her, then just pause at her name and reflect. Within moments, seconds even, you'll be smiling as you realize that not only is she in the second group of life travelers mentioned above, she's organizing and leading the group. You may have just heard her voice in your head. You've seen her enter a room and instantly draw attention. You know her take charge; get it done, "ninety-nine-and-a-half won't do" tenacity. You've heard her encourage, inspire and command. You know that even when life trips her up, she's never down for long and she's going to turn around and give some kind of blessing to whatever tripped her. For you, this book will remind you of why you love her and count it a privilege to call her friend.

If you don't know her, then you're about to meet an extraordinary woman of courage, boldness and faith. She's a woman who was determined to walk with God through the deepest valley and darkest storm of her life even while she could see no reason why it should happen. And walk with God she did. Heartache wasn't new for Rachelle. She'd already experienced unspeakable trauma against her before experiencing the tragedy she writes about in these pages. That trauma did not destroy her and neither would this tragedy. Neither what was done to her nor what was taken from her was able to defeat what was deep within her; her faith in a Sovereign God.

As a single mother with shattered dreams, raising three children, Rachelle could have easily fallen into the trap of self-pity and complacency that many do. But self-pity was never an option for Rachelle. She's always known she was destined to something greater, no matter how hard she had to fight to reach it. *She's supposed to be famous!* So living in defeat or complacency was not something she would allow for herself, her children or anyone around her. Rachelle is a fighter in spirit. She doesn't fight with words or fists. She fights with faith. She presses in trust. She pushes forward in hope. She keeps walking; one step at a time, through valleys, deserts, over mountains, in times of joy or sorrow, pressing toward the prize of the higher calling that she knows is hers in Jesus Christ.

I'm so very honored to write the foreword to Rachelle's book. I'm not famous...*yet* (an inside joke between Rachelle and me). So if you're asking who I am, the answer is, I'm just a friend. I'm a friend who has watched Rachelle's dogged determination to live her faith in every circumstance and find a lesson in every situation. For her, it's never enough to just get through something. She must turn and help whoever else might be facing the same or similar challenge. That's why you're holding this book in your hands. For Rachelle, part of the victory in going through what she has and continues to live through, is sharing what she's learned so that someone else's journey is easier.

I pray that as you read Rachelle's story and hear her heart, you will be encouraged to press through the unexplainable battles in your life, determined to walk in faith with the Sovereign God who may not give you a reason for the terror you face, but who can and will bring triumph if you will fix your eyes on Him. Rachelle has learned to look for His hand, lean on His heart and listen for His whisper. May we all be blessed to learn the same.

Christi C Evans

Rachelle Law

PREFACE

There was a time it bothered me to receive a compliment in front of other people because I felt it left them feeling inferior. That was the little extra-critical voice in my head externalizing that I was not good enough and maybe even undeserving. But over the years I realized those compliments were acknowledgments of my value. There was no need to undermine my self-confidence; instead, I would reinforce it. I decided no longer to demean my achievements; I would encourage them. And through it all I learned it is okay to shine. I became determined to let nothing dim the light that shined within me.

As a single mother, I found myself at the center of controversy that shaped my belief system and made me think differently. No matter what anyone else thought, if I found something worthy I gave my best efforts, sacrifice, and tears to it. And I encouraged my three extraordinary children never to quit.

I dedicate this book to single mothers everywhere who find themselves in a tight spot, backed in a corner with a room full of doubt with the desire to quit. At some point in our lives, we get to a place where we feel like giving up. Sometimes we give up before we even start, and other times we give up just before we are about to make the huge breakthrough that we have been putting so much effort into achieving. The only valid excuse you have for quitting is being dead. As long as you are alive, you have the choice to keep trying until you finally succeed.

Everyone has been touched by the loss of someone. And while we all grieve in a different way, I believe you never get over the loss in your heart. Yes, you get through the important milestones—the first birthday, first holiday, and the first cookout without the presence of the missing loved one. But even after there has been time for everyday life to be reestablished, the pain can be intense. I believe you have to acknowledge the fact that, when you love someone and that person is gone; you're going to miss him or her. And that has nothing to do with your spiritual strength or if you trust in God. It's a perfectly natural thing to continue to miss someone who has died.

My Whisper from God is a mother's journal about a son who died much too early. It is risky for me to share my deepest thoughts this way, but the greater misfortune would be for me not to share. This book is a deep expression of love, confidence, and transparency. *My Whisper from God* shares how quitting was not an option. How I learned to acknowledge his death without ever forgetting him and his charming ways. How I moved on without him and finally let go of the heartache and sorrow.

It is amazing how things of great significance can start in such an insignificant way and change your life forever—events that will devastate you and make you question everything. This book will not make you forget about your loss, but will help you to appreciate what you gain.

I took another walk around the neighborhood and realized that on this earth as it is

The race is not always to the swift,
nor the battle to the strong,
nor satisfaction to the wise
nor riches to the smart,
nor grace to the learned.
Sooner or later bad luck hits us all.

Ecclesiastes 9:11, the Message (MSG)

PROLOGUE

When I was sixteen years old, I was in the tenth grade. The world was my oyster and life was good — full of endless possibilities. I made my mark in my bell-bottom jeans and my afro, a child of the seventies bred on Earth, Wind & Fire, the Commodores, and Parliament Funkadelic's "Flashlight." It was a time of innocence.

It was a time when Soul Train was the show to watch on Saturday morning after completing my chores. There was no Internet. To find information, you went to the library or looked it up in an encyclopedia. It was a time when going to the movies was a rare treat and a birthday with candles, cake and family was enough. It was a time free of the fear of AIDS, free of drive-by shootings, free of so many of the problems that plague us today. I had a loving family with two brothers and two sisters. I was a cheerleader, looking forward to going off to college. I was on the right path. Life couldn't be better.

It's funny how friendship can end up in love. It was our first day back to school after summer vacation and I felt I had met the love of my life. Clarence was good looking, the epitome of tall, dark, and handsome. Our friendship grew out of our individuality, our strengths, and our weaknesses. There were good times and times when he irked me.

Clarence was intriguing. Maybe it was his laugh or his bad-boy tendencies. Though as a young girl I was trained to stay away from bad boys, training doesn't always stick, and in some ways it went against nature. Clarence had untamed masculinity, freedom, and smooth confidence that drew me to him. He was even more interesting outside of class. He was quiet, but there was an adventurous side that I found enticing.

We dated for a while. We had a good and intimate friendship; puppy love is what some would call it. Whatever it was, I enjoyed being in it. I wanted us to forever be friends, but we began to believe we were in love. There is one thing about love: it does not always end up with friendship.

I had completely fallen for Clarence. I learned a little about myself in our relationship, especially that I loved hard; I give of myself completely. Nothing anyone says or thinks stands in my way.

We felt at ease when we talked to each other. I enjoyed his conversation and his sense of humor. Our first kiss was soft and sensual. When he hugged me, I wanted him never to let me go. Even in our silence, our relationship was perfect almost fairytale-like.

I became pregnant. I went from one child to three within three years. My life had become very complicated; something simple as holding hands became difficult. When there were two children, I had a hand for each, but when the third child came along, I struggled. Yet I grew while sharing my life one adventure at a time with three amazing children.

Several years later, within the span of a year, Clarence and I were married and divorced. The journey I had imagined had spun completely out of control. The relationship quickly turned into a rerun of Ike and Tina's. I "moved on." Independence was frightening with three children, but no more frightening than my freedom. I no longer desired to hide the truth. I found out burying and denying the truth about the man I thought I loved was trouble. His secrets affected me, affected the way I thought, acted, and spoke. My ambitions collapsed. He was not worthy of me. In time, I rose above my ignorance, worked hard, and soon I no longer saw him through rose-colored glasses. I decided never do things to look better in the eyes of someone else. No longer did I look to others for approval, to provide a sense of who I am.

Life can be very complicated after divorce. What troubled me the most was the other relationships I lost when my marriage fell apart. People I thought to be family just drifted away without any real condolence or understanding. In fact, some of them criticized me. I sought out all types of jobs, but mobility in the job market was limited. Eventually I enrolled in school and received my certification as a medical assistant. This would allow me to take care of my children without depending on their father.

My firstborn, Michele, is compassionate and giving. She has smooth, cocoa-brown skin, and dark-brown hair. She is breathtakingly beautiful with great cheekbones, a captivating smile, and soulful eyes. She stands five feet five inches tall. I often put Michele in charge of her siblings at an early age. She learned to be *the responsible one*. As the older sister, Michele took on more and more care-giving roles as she grew up.

Then there was Willie, paper-sack brown, confident, naturally caring, warm, whimsical, elegant, and charismatic. He had a Colgate smile, almond eyes, and beautiful, full, dark eyebrows. At six two, Willie was tall and very protective of his sisters—and even more protective of me. He completed everything he started and strived to be the best. He was a well-rounded athlete, participating in baseball, basketball, football, and track, yet when people share memories they speak of his character. Willie taught me about myself. Willie challenged me from the very beginning. He brought a different spin to the family, being the only boy. Willie valued good friendship and family.

Last but not least there is Ashley, who has a charming smile and is quick to listen and slow to speak, determined, and a hard worker. She has brown skin and the same height as her sister. She has pronounced cheekbones, a chiseled chin, and she is somewhat reclusive. Yet she has a laugh that could shake a room.

My children have been a gift to each other as much as they have been a gift to me. That is probably why they learned to rely on each other and I trusted them to do so.

Because I spent eleven years in major league baseball as an assistant to the vice president of marketing and in sales, it's easy for me to compare life to baseball. Baseball, we know, is exact, traditional. It's a world bound by foul lines, marked by fixed positions. The playing field is carefully laid out to the inch and cautiously statistical, while the game itself is a linear equation of batters retired and runs batted in. It begins with a song that has been slaughtered by some of the best vocalists and ends with the rasping whispers of "Maybe next time."

The story of my life is a lot like baseball. It is about learning how to meet the enemy head on, run the bases, and head back home, there to be greeted by those who love me unconditionally. That's baseball.

But life is different. For one thing, we live wherever we can, preferably in the best neighborhoods, connected by city streets and avenues. We live by choosing sides, arguing over who is the best. Until someone reminds us, "its life," we come close to throwing in the towel because of a bad call or because we have struck out. But we are reminded it's how we play the game that really matters.

Every now and then, life throws a curve ball. It's good to know the rules: three strikes you're out and four balls means you are sent walking. Of course, the lessons you learn last a lifetime. There were times when the seasons of my life would be so long, I was convinced I had been chosen for the wrong team. I even considered quitting. As in baseball, I had to learn to trust the Coach in life. And I learned it after many innings, strike- outs, and unanticipated walks.

CHAPTER 1

Injustice anywhere is a threat to justice everywhere.
~ Martin Luther King,
African -American civil rights leader

For the righteous LORD *loves justice. The virtuous will see his face. ~ Psalm 11:7*
New Living Translation (NLT)

Chapter 1

On that summer afternoon, July 2, 1996, on an Independence Day weekend — a celebration of every person's right to life, liberty, and the pursuit of happiness — Willie's rights were violated and denied.

Rights can't be taken away, which is not to say that they can't be violated or denied. While I believe these rights are common to all humankind, the truth is, they can be and often are denied to each one of us. On that warm summer day, Willie's rights were sacrificed.

Willie was tall, thin, and soft spoken. As most young men going through puberty, his voice was changing and had started to crack. He spoke in a whisper, deep and slow. He was confident and a young man of few words. But his laugh was boisterous. When he walked into a room, you could not help but notice him. He could always put a smile on my face. He was intelligent, resilient, ambitious, and affectionate. Willie was looking forward to being a member of the freshman football team at Hickman Mills High School in the fall. Hickman was a predominately white high school at the time. He had been encouraged to attend conditioning training to become stronger and faster for the upcoming football season. He was dressed in typical workout attire, which was clothing he would be comfortable in—nothing too loose or too tight.

Willie was new to the school and didn't know what to expect. He was anxious to meet the members of the football team. He was scheduled to attend orientation in a few weeks before school actually started. The orientation would help him to learn his way around the building and to meet fellow freshmen.

Hickman was about three and a half miles away from our apartment complex in South Kansas City. He was new to the area and would be walking alone. Willie did not mind the walk, but I preferred to drive him. It was a pretty simple route, yet there was potential for danger on foot. It was either an eight- to ten-minute ride or a forty-five-minute walk.

That morning I decided I would give him a ride. I dropped Willie off at the entrance of the high school before going to work. I had given him the normal reminders that I did every day. I told him I loved him, and I told him to be careful and to remember whose he was. This was a little saying of mine, a way of reminding my children who they were in Christ. I wanted them to remember that their life should glorify Christ.

I sat in my car and watched him go inside. I pulled off slowly and headed toward the interstate to work. I had given Willie pocket money just in case his ride did not show. He could catch a taxi home or provide gas money if someone was willing to give him a ride.

I knew I could not be with my children 24/7, but I made it a point to give them as much guidance as possible to help keep them safe. I was adamant about them being aware of their surroundings. It did not make a difference how old they were; it never hurt to reiterate the dangers lurking. Despite their protests I continued to offer my advice, even if I was not sure they were listening.

Willie made a stop in the boy's restroom before going to the weight room. While washing his hands, he was approached by an off-duty police sergeant. He was Caucasian, overweight, and had black hair except for the bald spot in the top of his head. He approached Willie and asked him, "What are you doing?" Willie told the officer he was there to lift weights. The sergeant then told Willie to get out of the restroom. Willie turned off the water and left the restroom.

Willie had been well informed as a young black male what his behavior should be if he was ever stopped by an officer. He knew that he must keep in mind that the officer believes he has a reason or probable cause to stop and ask him anything. He knew to collect his thoughts and remain calm. He was to say as little as possible, and he knew the officer was to respect his rights. He knew not to answer any questions that sounded accusatory. Willie followed the orders of the officer. He left the restroom and proceeded toward the weight room. Little did he know at that moment he had been targeted by the police and what was ahead of him.

Willie was born December 1, 1981, and named Clarence Willard Smith Jr. He accumulated several nicknames in his lifetime. As a young boy, he was called Lil' Man or Willie by family members. Then there was C-Dub, once he reached high school, and later he was referred to as Whisper.

Willie met life head-on with confidence and did not depend on social approval. He liked to be original and did not mind doing it alone. He was a clear thinker, decisive, and self-assured. When inspired by an idea, he executed. He was not a follower.

Willie was born into a family full of strong women. He was the only boy sandwiched between two sisters, Michele and Ashley. He recognized early on that he was here for a purpose, but he did not go looking for it. He was self-confident and knew his purpose lay within. He was not concerned about being accepted or what other people thought his purpose should be.

Because of his warm and friendly nature, he never met a stranger. He was destined to touch many lives along the way. He encouraged and supported "the least of them." He took advantage of each and every opportunity God provided, whether it was at school, church, or on the streets. Willie was aware of his gifts and talents and knew what he wanted in life. And he attracted circumstances and people consistent to his desires.

I made it a point to support Willie in God's purpose in his life. When I took him to the movies or other outings, I relentlessly posed questions and encouraged conversation. He was provided with positive and negative criticism not only from me but also from others who played an important role in his life. I made it my responsibility to have Willie attend school and church, where he was introduced to great teachers and mentors who imparted wisdom, direction, and purpose into his life.

As Willie continued with his first day of conditioning, he felt a supreme sense of satisfaction and looked forward to preparation for tryouts. He always felt good pushing his body further than he thought it could go. After completing his weight sets and repetitions that day, he signed out and headed toward the front exit. While waiting for his ride, he reflected on his first day and the camaraderie in the weight room. The same officer approached him, but he was not alone this time. He had a companion, a young Caucasian officer.

The sergeant walked over to Willie and flipped Willie's hat with his hand, almost knocking it off his head. The sergeant then asked Willie how old he was. Willie responded fourteen. With no specific reason, the sergeant took hold of him and placed him under arrest for "trespassing."

Willie's visit to the school was legitimate, and he was indeed waiting for a ride. He had not been asked to leave the building. He had not made any disturbance. He had informed the officer of his reason for being at the school. The actions of the officer had nothing to do with Willie's age or if he was authorized to be there. The officer had his own agenda. He didn't escort Willie out of the bathroom or verify with the staff on duty that Willie should be there.

The officer had sought Willie out. The incident could have been avoided had the officer verified the information Willie provided. But he had no intention of verifying it, because he had a plan of his own, a premeditated plan. The officer was flexing his muscles and abusing his authority. His behavior alone let me know this was not the first time he had done this. He was a repeat defender of racial profiling. My son of fourteen had been placed under arrest and treated as a common criminal.

A young Black male waiting for his ride home, Willie had been singled out and subjected to scrutiny just because of his race. That's an ugly charge. My son had been unofficially introduced to his first dirty cop. Yes, a dirty cop. I call it the way I see it. A spade is a spade. This incident painted a crystal-clear picture and altered my perception of police officers. I had no desire to even talk to a police officer. And just the thought of this incident aggravates me still.

I think of all the young Black boys and possibly Black girls who have been or will be subjected to similar treatment by a police officer. Seeing the corruption of the police, citizens are likely to lose respect for them where it really counts — namely, in their capacity as crime fighters. Police officers often need the help of citizens in fighting crime, but this help is not likely to be forthcoming from a citizen that lacks respect for police officers who have mistreated those in the community.

No one cares about your child's future more than you do. And there is one thing you cannot get back once it is gone: your child's innocence. What had started out as one of many firsts in high school had turned into a day to remember for all the wrong reasons.

Both officers put their hands in Willie's pockets, and

the sergeant removed the money Willie had there: $9.35. As the officer pulled the money from his pocket, the officer said, "Business is good." Willie said nothing. I am certain the sergeant was trying to get a rise out of him, but Willie said nothing, praise God. The young officer requested Willie's name, address, and phone number as well as my work number. Willie obliged, but the officer never used the information to contact me.

The sergeant asked the younger officer to call a paddy wagon. It was my understanding paddy wagons were called for when "prisoners" were resisting arrest or if the officer might be attacked in a patrol car. Well, there was no resistance, and multiple officers were not called. This was a fourteen-year-old with no prior record.

The younger officer didn't agree, so he called dispatch back and requested a police car. In a short time, the paddy wagon had arrived—likely dispatched from the Hickman Patrol. The sergeant stood Willie in front of the car door and then led him to the paddy wagon. The driver of the paddy wagon removed the cuffs, placed a different set of handcuffs on Willie, and placed him in the paddy wagon.

CHAPTER 2

Never be bullied into silence. Never allow yourself to be made a victim. Accept no one's definition of your life; define yourself.
~ Harvey Fierstein

It's wrong, very wrong, to go along with injustice.
~ Proverbs 24:23
The Message (MSG)

Chapter 2

This pre-football experience could have easily changed Willie's mind-set and discouraged him from returning to the school, but *the devil is a liar*. Willie had done nothing wrong. He would get through this. He was determined to play football, and he would play. When he went after something, he gave it his all. Not to say he didn't get discouraged, because he did. But he would not allow it to fester.

With all the injustice in the world, it is hard not to hold a grudge. We expect fairness, but often we get just the opposite. Grudges are heavy, and if we are not able to forgive and to let go of the heaviness of these feelings, they wear us out and eat away at our peace of mind.

Imagine being a fourteen-year-old with no history of

trouble, having never experienced a run-in with the police or the juvenile court system, and now you are being arrested at the school you are enrolled to attend in the fall on grounds of trespassing—even though the records indicated you signed in and had been lifting weights.

Willie could at times have issues when being closed into tiny places for an extended period. Only the grace of God allowed him to endure the ride. The driver of the paddy wagon drove around and then pulled up to a building with a gray door. Willie said all he could see was a gray door. He was a very observant child and tried to stay alert in order to identify where he was. The driver pulled into a garage for a moment, and Willie heard the door open and close. The driver got out of the paddy wagon and then got back in the paddy wagon, and then Willie was driven to the Juvenile Center.

Upon arriving there, Willie was asked the same questions the young officer had asked him while on school grounds: name, address, and phone numbers. This was the second time the information was requested, yet there was no effort made to contact me, his mother.

A different officer appeared and took Willie's shoe strings, his hat, and his money—the infamous $9.35. A gentleman in plain clothes asked Willie, "Why are you here?" Willie responded, "The officers said trespassing." He went on to explain that he had arrived at the school to take advantage of the weight room. Willie said pictures were taken and he was placed in a cell.

The officer on duty placed a call to the arresting officer. When he completed the call, he hung up the receiver and told Willie that the arresting officer had told a different story. He then encouraged Willie to change his story so that it matched the officer's story. The police officer became adamant about Willie recanting what he said had happened. Maybe that is why I was not called. It was their attempt to force a fourteen-year-old to agree to something he didn't do. Willie shared with me that he responded to the police officer by saying, "Does that make the police officer automatically right?" The officer said yes. It was all so unbelievable: not only had he been handcuffed and placed in a paddy wagon, but also pressured to change his story.

According to Missouri law when a law enforcement officer takes a juvenile into custody, the officer must read the juvenile his Miranda rights and provide the juvenile the right to call an attorney. Willie was not permitted to make any calls. As it states in the report, the information was requested from him on two accounts. It was not until late afternoon that I received a phone call, and the voice on the other end was not my son. It was an officer who asked if I knew my son was at Juvenile Detention. And of course I didn't know, and before he asked the question he knew, because there was no record of

Willie being offered the opportunity to call.

The gentleman on the phone proceeded to inform me he had just arrived for his shift, and he noticed Willie was there in a cell. What would have happened had he not "noticed" Willie being there? Really! There had been a shift change, and obviously there was no communication in regards to a fourteen-year-old being held in a cell. No one bothered to make certain his guardian had been notified of his whereabouts.

Never giving it a second thought, I had no reason to believe my son was not home. I had dropped him off that morning and headed to work. Now I had received a call from the Juvenile office notifying me he had been arrested. I was in disbelief, frightened of what could have taken place in that godforsaken place. It took all I had to remain calm until I could leave work and get to the dreaded Juvenile Center.

I am certain they ran a report to see if there was a history of priors, especially since the arresting officer insinuated drugs were involved. Of course, there was not. I was not familiar with the procedure of the police department, but I knew without a shadow of a doubt the policy and procedures were not being followed that day. Being there were no priors, maybe they felt they would start a "rap" sheet. Now, keep in mind that Willie could have easily been taken to the patrol office in the area, but he was taken clear downtown and encouraged to change his story. He was stripped of his dignity and placed in a cell.

I arrived at the doors to the Juvenile Center and walked toward the officer at the desk with fire in my eyes. As nice as I could, I asked for my son. I waited as my mind raced to a thousand different places. What had happened to him while he was in their custody? It was obvious they could care less. What would they say if he had died in their custody? Their shift had ended, and they had gone home to be with their families, possibly their sons. The police officers had been so insensitive, uncaring. No remorse was shown.

After what seemed like an eternity, my son walked out of the cell. On first glance, he appeared to be completely drained. My heart sunk as I moved to greet him. I hugged him and would not allow myself to cry. I would not give them the satisfaction, but I eyed each and every one in the room. This was not the end of this matter. I was thoroughly disgusted with the police department for what had transpired.

As I hugged Willie, I could tell that a lot had changed in those hours. I finally managed to stop hugging him. Looking into his sad eyes, I couldn't explain away what had taken place. I wanted an explanation and found none. Everyone seemed to have passed the buck. I did not want to overwhelm him with my questions, because I was sure mentally he had been there and back. I wanted to know what was going on in his head and what had gone on while he was in that paddy wagon, in that cell. I was getting irritated the more I stood in the middle of the floor. One thing I did know is this: if you are brought to it, you will be brought through it.

Rachelle Law

CHAPTER 3

You're either part of the solution or part of the problem.
~ (Leroy) Eldridge Cleaver

If you let people treat you like a doormat, you'll be quite
forgotten in the end. ~ Proverbs 29:21
The Message (MSG)

Chapter 3

I didn't go straight home. I needed some male support. I have two brothers, and the oldest lived in the Hickman Mills District. That's where I headed. As I drove down the highway, allowing Willie some time to unwind to the best of his ability, I was very selective in choosing my words. I questioned him and he was clear and to the point. He answered each and every question I posed. He never once stuttered. I did not realize how long we had been talking until I realized we had arrived at my brother's home. Bobby and his wife, Rhonda, were home. I began to share the incident that had taken place as they stared in disbelief.

My brother had a pool in his backyard. He suggested Willie change into a pair of trunks and go for a swim. Willie swam lap after lap, and with each lap he released some of the weight that lay heavily on his heart and his mind. After swimming numerous consecutive laps, he rested at the side of the pool. As he looked off into the distance, I knew he was replaying the day over in his head. I walked out on to the second-floor deck of my brother's house, and in that moment I was more determined than ever to do all I could to be the voice that he'd lost when this whole ordeal began.

On July 8, 1996, Willie and I filed a citizen complaint about the incident. I received a letter on July 10, 1996, informing us it would be forwarded to the Internal Affairs Unit for a "complete investigation." That was followed by a letter dated July 15, 1996, implying the filed complaint had been forwarded to the Internal Affairs Unit of the police department's investigation unit. The letter stated that in order to proceed with the investigation, Willie needed to provide a formal statement. That was not a difficult task at all. It would be difficult only if you had something to hide or if you had something to lie about, but neither was the case. I arranged to take off work, and we both reported to the Internal Affairs Unit so Willie could tell what happened. He recalled the incident from beginning to end, and I sat there with him as he told the truth about the alleged trespassing.

Every member on that board from A to Z failed us, especially the sergeant that tried to destroy my son. The younger police officer stood by, knowing he could have made a difference, but chose to buckle and not take a stand. I have never looked at the police department the same since. There were some prominent people on that board. When I received the results of the "investigation," the thought of that board sickened me to the very core. The letter implied Willie's incident would remain on file. As long as Willie was not involved in any future delinquencies, the incident would be removed from their records. Some investigation. Never once did they call to ask questions or ask to meet the young man they discarded. But what was meant for bad was orchestrated by God for Willie's good.

That summer came to a close, and on the first day of his freshman year, Willie walked through the doors of Hickman Mills High School and did not allow what happened that summer to hinder him from his destiny. The system that was established to protect him, had made no effort to support him, but what God had for him was for him. He was able to live and love with no regrets. He made the football team and lettered in football each year.

Willie had indeed overcome yet another situation that only catapulted him to the next level. If he didn't know anything else, he knew he was loved. There are so many young men who have gone and may still be going up against injustice on a daily basis. As unfortunate as it is, there are young boys in the system, not because they are guilty, but because there is someone who took an oath and without hesitation didn't honor it. So if you are a young man or a family member of someone who was stripped of their innocence, do not give up.

It may appear that Willie lost the battle, but in losing it, he gained courage to take a stand. He could have easily chosen not to file the complaint, but in that moment he knew he wasn't alone and that I had his back. So, what often appears as a loss to some is really a win. He learned how to go through an experience and how to react. He exemplified lessons he had been taught in his early years. The encounter was not in vain. What was meant for bad was in the end for his good.

I instilled in my children that giving up is not an option. Anyone can give up; it's the easiest thing in the world to do. The desire to quit happens often. Sometimes the voices in our culture urge us to throw in the towel and to give up. But to hold it together when everyone else would understand if you fell apart is true strength.

I remind my children daily whose image they were made in despite, what the world says. Often their father was not around, and male mentors were few and far between. Without male mentors, many men of this generation have felt lost, unsure of how to deal with an unspeakable lack in their lives. A male mentor in my son's life after this incident could not be underestimated. No matter how I wanted to see things from Willie's viewpoint, even I could not fully understand how it was to be a young boy. I had never experienced what he experienced or would experience the pressures and cultural expectations of a Black male. Whether the situation is right, wrong, or fair is beside the point. He needed someone he could connect to, identify with, and talk to about things that are outside the realm of a woman's experience.

CHAPTER 4

*Success is to be measured not so much by the position
that one has reached in life as by the obstacles which he
has overcome while trying to succeed.
~ Booker T. Washington (1856-1915)*

*My sons, obey your father's commands, and don't
neglect your mother's instruction. ~ Proverbs 6:20
New Living Translation (NLT)*

Chapter 4

If you really want something, you must go for it despite the obstacles. Some battles are a little harder to win. Then again, you will never see what the end is going to be if you give up. Those who knew Willie may have thought his life was uncomplicated, because he wore a great big smile. But he overcame great difficulties. He lived a fulfilling life and had some great moments, but had he given up all those who were inspired by his triumphs may not have overcome their own struggles. Willie's motivation was absolutely compelling. I credit him for knowing who he was.

He was someone who did not entertain naysayers. Telling Willie he couldn't accomplish something was like giving him a vote that he could. He knew what he wanted, and nothing would keep him from whatever he set his mind to accomplish.

Willie was very involved in youth activities at church. He managed to win several accolades at church as well as at school. He gave of himself. You could find Willie reading to students at the elementary school. He was a giver, and it is true that when you give with the right motives, it is reciprocated.

I expected great things from Willie, and he knew it. He may not have had the material things that many other kids had, but he would take what he had and make the best of it. For example, I wasn't one to buy shoes because someone's name was on it. I did not understand why I should pay more for Willie's tennis shoes than what I would pay for my shoes, when I was the one working for those dollars. So Willie would mark his tennis shoes up and brand them. He was creative.

I believe Willie understood my thinking on that subject; although he may not have agreed, he understood. We talked about money and the lack of it in our home. So when his tennis shoes were stolen out of his locker and he came home shoeless, I almost went crazy. You better believe I made a trip to the school and called out all the young boys in the locker room. That is just a small example of what I would do for my son. He was my only son, and in no uncertain terms I declared it.

Willie was a modest and charming individual. He

became friends with many girls during puberty. Even though he was comfortable having them as just friends, it was not long before he began to see girls beyond friendship.

If you were to ask my children one characteristic about me, they would probably unanimously say I have a need to teach. I believe you can learn from every situation, and with every opportunity I found a teaching moment. I was aware of my influence, and even though at the time I was a youth director at church, I made a conscious effort to start at home. I knew I had the best classroom in the world under my roof. What took place there would evolve into what they would become in life.

The time came when Willie wanted to talk about dating. I hadn't always made good decisions in that area, so I was truthful with him and discussed what I would have done differently if given another chance. Then there were times I made some good decisions, and I shared with him why I thought they were good.

As a single parent, I had become accustomed to attending movies alone. Not many people appreciate the same things I do, and when I wanted to go, I wanted to go. Sometimes it is easier to make last-minute plans when you don't have someone else to consider. Yes, it is fun to share movie experiences with a friend, but if I waited until someone agreed to go, I would miss out on many opportunities.

There were times when special events would come along, and I would find myself dateless by choice. Why waste a good evening on a bad date when I had a son who could be exposed to new things? In November 1997, I had a teaching moment. I had an opportunity to attend the opening of the Negro League Baseball Museum on Eighteenth and Vine. This was my opportunity to have a date with my son and implement one of the lessons I learned from Brother George.

Willie would need a tuxedo. He didn't have one, and there was only one person I could think of to help me — my younger brother, Darren, who was very selective in his attire. I called him, even though I was sure he would have loved to attend. Darren was a superlative baseball player and just as big of a fan. He was an outstanding first baseman and pitcher. He didn't hesitate, and he didn't ask if I had an extra ticket. He could see how important this was for Willie and me. He had a tuxedo that fit Willie; it was not a custom fit, but it would do.

I was excited and looked forward to my son, who once played baseball himself, attending an event as grand as this would be. We took several pictures before leaving home and found ourselves in the company of many dignitaries that evening, such as Danny Glover and Kareem Abdul-Jabbar. Willie was tall himself, but when he stood next to Kareem, he seemed to come to Kareem's waist. Then there was Bob Costas, who before taking the stage took the time to shake Willie's hand. Willie never forgot the evening. Willie was happy that he attended and for the opportunity to meet so many people. He embraced the opportunity and was able to see what was within his reach. He felt that he too could be a dignitary. Why not?

At one point in the evening, he asked me about a couple who was being a little frisky and acting a bit inappropriate at the table. I was glad he noticed and was thankful for the opportunity to teach. It was the perfect opening to discuss the dos and don'ts of dating. Making certain to leave no stone unturned, I answered his questions and concerns. He continued to survey the room, which provided more questions. I was direct and honest as I answered each question.

I am certain that when he reflected on that night, several things came to mind: the movie stars, the athletes, the commentators, and the couple at our table, whose behavior allowed Willie and me to share in one of the most important conversations we had. I still think about that night and how good he looked in his tuxedo and how proud I was to be escorted on one of the best dates in my life.

I will always remember my son's first official date. I learned so much from him that evening. He confirmed that although I doubted he was listening, he was. It encouraged me to stay the course, because even when I felt I was talking to a brick wall, he was listening. I knew he was on the right track. And when he decided to date formally, I knew he would be the kind of young man I would trust with someone else's daughters.

Willie was a very thoughtful young man. He was the kind of guy who would sacrifice his last even to a stranger. The weekend before my 40th birthday a lovely bouquet of flowers arrived at my job. I wasn't dating anyone, so imagine the look on my face when the flowers arrived. I began to read the card and I realized it was from the most important man in my life; my son. I love fresh flowers. The flowers caused a stir with my coworkers. They spoke of how handsome Willie was and how special it must be to have a son that would send flowers. I was grateful, but Willie was only a senior in high school and he didn't have a credit card. It isn't customary to have flowers delivered without a credit card. Being the mother I was, I wondered how he managed such an awesome surprise.

After finally reaching him by phoned I told him how he had made my day. Before he hung up the phone I asked him how he was able to order the flowers. He said, "Ms. Gordon." Ms. Gordon was the assistant principal at Hickman Mills' high school. Willie expressed his desire to send me flowers, but he needed a credit card. She was so overwhelmed that he was willing to spend his money in such a special way she agreed to use her credit card. He gave her the cash he had set aside for my birthday. Willie sending flowers was the highlight of my 40th birthday.

It was Willie's senior year and basketball season. He had been staying late after school each day for tryouts. He had spent many of his summer hours playing on a team for the basketball coach. As we were sitting in the living room, Willie walked in the front door, not his normal self. He motioned with his fist balled and with one finger extended across the base of his neck as his head hung low. I was not sure what he was referring to, so he motioned again and said he had been cut from the team. I was floored. How could he be cut when he had played well for three consecutive years? It goes without saying how devastated he was with the news. He took it pretty hard and understandably so. This was not the first time seniors had been cut by that coach.

I was not going to take this sitting down. I wanted answers. A meeting was called, but the coach never explained his decision and abruptly left the meeting. The athletic director was in attendance and did not stop the coach from leaving, not that it would have made a difference. What was done was done, and it was heartbreaking for Willie as well as for me to watch him go through it. This was one of those times his father showed up and because he did, what came out of this meant the world to Willie.

There were so many times his spirit was broken, but he never gave up. He recalled the stories of successful athletes who never gave up, which encouraged him to believe in himself.

Limitations and roadblocks are placed in your life for you to overcome them. They are not there for you to whine and complain. Willie's life was a never-ending testimony, as he constantly had to push past the impossible, regardless of what it looked like, and even when things were not what they appeared to be. He was not the kind of person to give in to what he couldn't do. As an athlete, you will only be limited by what you believe is possible. Willie trusted what was given to him naturally; what he lacked, he trained to get. His goals motivated him.

I believe that if you allow your children to quit anything they will become quitters. Every time an obstacle comes, it will become easier and easier for them to quit. When you quit, you give up before you even start. Or you give up just before you are about to get that huge breakthrough you had been putting so much effort toward. So I encouraged Willie never to quit. He always gave it his all. But this situation was out of his hands. It was not easy for him, but as a family, we prayed God's will be done, and it was well with our souls.

It took Willie some time to get over this particular obstacle. It broke his spirit, but he never gave up his love for the game. I loved the game because I had spent so much time watching and playing with him. He continued to play ball on the block with friends and family, but no longer played organized basketball.

CHAPTER 5

The battles that count aren't the ones for gold medals.
The struggles within yourself – the invisible, inevitable
battles inside all of us - that's where it's at.
~ Jesse Owens (1913-1980)

"Physical training is good, but training for godliness is
much better, promising benefits in this life and in the
life to come." ~ I Timothy 4:8
New Living Translation (NLT)

Chapter 5

Track season was upon us, and Willie set his sights on a track championship. He had more time to train since he was not on the basketball team. An unexpected injury was an early headache for Willie. He had injured his leg during the football season, and it had begun to give him some trouble. It was the same leg that had been hit by a car when he was younger. However, he was determined to run track his last year of high school. There were good days and bad days as he struggled with his leg injury. He never stopped believing that he would overcome and qualify to compete at the state track meet.

I continued to believe in God's mercy, compassion, and healing power. There was no doubt Willie would be healed. I knew many stories in the Bible, such as the one about the woman with the issue of blood and the two blind men. I knew enough to know it was their faith in Jesus that made them whole. And if we had anything, we had faith. God had been faithful in other life circumstances. I also am familiar with the story in the Bible about Paul, who begged three times to be healed, but God told him His grace is sufficient. So, even if God chose not to heal Willie's leg, we trusted Him.

One Sunday morning at the closing of the church's annual women's retreat, Willie received his healing. The Spirit was high. The Shekinah glory was present, and God's glory was in the house. The guest evangelist and special retreat guest was Dr. Loretta McIntosh. She had been preaching on standing in the gap (Ezekiel 22:30). That particular day, she stood in the gap as an intercessor on my son's behalf. She invited people from the congregation to come up for prayer. Willie went forward, and she drew him in closer and began to minister to him. I was not close enough to hear, although I wish I was.

Willie stared directly into her face and listened intensely. Dr. McIntosh instructed him to run, and Willie did not question her instructions. He received prayer, and he believed he was healed, so he began to run around the sanctuary. If there was anyone present who doubted the power of prayer or thought healing no longer existed, that doubt disappeared that morning, and they became a believer. Our entire church family experienced a miracle.

Many may have thought that Willie's leg was injured for good, but God said differently. Willie was competing again with no problem and had begun to win his races. Before long he had qualified to compete at the state track meet in Jefferson City. Willie had some of the greatest track coaches: Ms. Woodson, Ms. Tantara, Coach Stairs, Coach Hurt, and then there was Coach Robinson, who had supported and encouraged Willie every step of the way.

Of course, Willie was excited he would be competing in the state track meet. He contacted his dad to share the news and to inform him when he would be competing. But he told Willie he wouldn't be able to attend. Willie was disappointed, but it did not change his desire to bring home the gold.

On the day of the state meet, Michele, Ashley, and I set out in a rental car. I headed out 71 South when we should have taken 70-East. Somehow and some way I was misdirected and almost missed his first race of the day. The girls were fuming. We took a few turns, and we were back on course. I understood their frustration. No one was more frustrated than me.

After a three-and-a-half-hour drive that should have been two and a half, we reached the university and could feel the excitement in the air. There were school buses, charter buses, and people on foot headed toward the track. This was not the first time we attended, but the first time I drove.

We were late, and I had no idea what race was taking place. I needed to find a parking spot and the sooner the better. We drove around for fifteen or twenty minutes before I noticed an empty spot in the grass over the hill, down the street from the stadium. I am a very excitable person and began to get loud and anxious. The girls laughed at me, but I did not mind. It was good to know they were speaking to me again.

We parked on a slight hill and began to walk uphill, following the noise of the cheering crowd. As we walked we could hear the announcer call for the runners for the 110 hurdles. We looked at each other and began to walk faster. I just had to get in the stands. I couldn't drive all this way and miss his race. My heart was pumping fast. And as I walked, I was getting short of breath.

We finally reached the entrance, paid our admission, and headed toward the bleachers. We had not gone ten feet when we ran into some of his track team members, which was a good sign. Had the race been taking place, they would have been in the bleachers cheering for him.

We made it just in the nick of time. Thank God! Everyone was asking what had taken us so long, and the girls were happy to give the reason for our tardiness. The stadium was packed, and it was good to know Brother George and his wife were there to support Willie. Brother George has always been supportive; he was a track star and held records while he was in college.

The hurdles were being set up, and I could not keep still. I could see Willie in the distance at the starting line. He was stretching and jumping as he always did. Then I heard the announcer telling the racers to take their marks. Willie crouched down in front of his blocks. He pressed the fingertips of his hands onto the track and extended one leg at a time to get securely positioned in the blocks. His head was down for a moment, which seemed like minutes. "On your mark," said the announcer. Willie rose up from his squatting position. His eyes were straight ahead. Then the gun went off.

Willie came out of the blocks like a racehorse. He ran like crazy. I found myself running down the bleachers as if I could run the race for him. As I ran, I yelled louder with each step. He had a sizeable lead. His sisters were screaming as loud as I was. The onlookers were going crazy. He took first place and would compete the following day in the finals.

I could not contain myself. I had released all that pent-up energy from that long drive and the fear of traveling that distance only to miss my son. But I did make it in time, and he had run like never before. He had run like a horse in the Kentucky Derby. We yelled his name and waved, letting him know we were there. He gave one glimpse of that smile that could light a darkened room. His smile said it all. He had accomplished what he had set out to do. Win!

The state track meet was such an exciting event. It was the chance to compete with all the other track teams throughout the state of Missouri, and many people were there to support their loved one. There were at least fifty to one hundred people for every track team. Each team walked around the track together displaying signs and chanting ditties; the solidarity was incredible. There was so much unity on the teams. There was nothing like it.

The first day had come to a close. Willie had qualified to run the 110 and the 300 intermediate hurdles. We stood outside talking about his races. He stood there smiling. Did I mention how humble he was? Whenever he played any sport, he was not the athlete to talk smack. He was cordial, respectful, and remained humble in the midst of competition. He was not the "I am the greatest" kind of winner. He was more of a "let my performance do the talking" young man.

The track team was staying in a different hotel than the girls and I. I had actually gotten a great deal on a parlor, though I knew nothing about a parlor. When I was making hotel reservations, Diana, a coworker, told me to request a parlor. I did what she said, and the woman on the other end made a few "let me see" comments and one or two "maybes." And then she said just what I wanted to hear: "Yes, the parlor is available." I had no idea where we would be staying. I just trusted Diana's judgment, because she knew I was seeking a nice, clean place on a tight budget.

We arrived at the hotel and checked into our parlor. It was a quaint room with a sofa sleeper and a small kitchen area, and it was very nicely decorated. It was perfect. We sat up most of the night talking about the races and how well Willie had run. No one could even remember that, early in the season, there was a chance Willie would not run, but there we were on the eve of the state finals in Jefferson City, and Willie was a qualifier.

I had the opportunity to speak to James Bell, a mentor who was staying in the same hotel as the athletes. He shared how Willie had spent the night before meditating and preparing not only physically but also mentally for the upcoming finals. He had gone off to be by himself because of all the distractions that were going on in the hotel, as well as his room. Willie was aware that it was a blessing to be there, and he was not going to allow any distractions to keep him from accomplishing what he had set out to do several months before.

The next morning we set out to win. We had breakfast and headed over to the university field. This was a big day in the state of Missouri. Today would determine the state's best in track and field.

Willie's first race came, and he found himself finishing in seventh place. He was distressed. He was over on the fence near the fans, very disappointed in himself. This was not the young man I knew, yet I understood his dissatisfaction in the outcome. But this was not the time to faint. I yelled out to him, "Pray! Pray!"

They presented medals to the top ten finishers, and Willie stood there showing no gratitude. I knew how badly he wanted to win the gold, but that did not justify his behavior. Regardless of how we feel, we are always ambassadors. I told him to put it behind him and reiterated how there were people who did not even medal. Eventually he pulled himself together and walked toward the starting line, but not in that order.

Willie had one race left that could change things around. I was on pins and needles as I waited in the stands for his race. He had on his game face, and he was stretching, not even looking at his competition. He was focused. He leaped in the air, the soles of his track shoes greeted each other midair, and then he landed with feet on the ground. He repeated this several times. I could only imagine how determined he was to place first.

He stepped into the blocks, and then the gun went off. Classmates, friends and family, and I were all screaming at the top of our lungs, "Run, Clarence!" using his birth name. Willie got to one of the hurdles and stumbled. I was not sure if his foot touched the hurdle or what happened, because there was something blocking our view. We all gasped and held our breath. And he recovered.

His longs legs continued to take strides around the first turn, making up time lost. He was dominating the race. It was now or never. This was his last race as a senior in high school. Our voices got louder, ear splittingly loud. The race was being taped, and I did not have the camera. I was banned from taping because I moved so much while I was holding the camera you could get motion sickness from watching the tape.

As Willie was taking the next turn, the number assigned to him fell off his track uniform. I could hear Big T, one of his teammates, saying "C-Dub ran out of his number." And one of Hickman coaches said, "Take him, Clarence!"

He was coming down the stretch. We were mesmerized as he crossed the finish line. He won! He was the winner with a time of 39:19. The second place winner came in at 39:39. The crowd was going wild. Clarence had stayed the course and had not given up despite his leg injury, discouragement, and even after placing seventh. He overcame them all. He was now the 2000 Division 3A boys 300-meter intermediate hurdles state champion. The 2000 Hickman Mills High School boy's track team placed first as a team in their division. We were all reminded that day that "being confident of this, that he who began a good work in you will carry it on to completion until the day of Christ Jesus." (Philippians 1:6).

Rachelle Law

CHAPTER 6

"Every choice in life either moves you forward or keeps you stuck."
~ Oprah Winfrey

Wise choices will watch over you. Understanding will keep you safe. ~ Proverbs 2:11
New Living Translation (NLT)

Chapter 6

The state meet was behind him, and there were only two things left to complete Willie's senior year: prom and graduation. Willie definitely had senioritis. He was trying to balance extracurricular activities, a social life, college preparation, and a part-time job. Somewhere along the way, homework had begun to seem less important; all he wanted to do was spend time with friends, which was his top priority.

Prior to graduation, Willie received many accolades, including being voted student of the year. The day of graduation was a day of blue skies and sunshine. With all the ups and downs, overall it had been a great year. Willie decided to accept the scholarship offer from William Jewell College, a four-year liberal arts college located in Liberty, Missouri. William Jewell had a long history of success through recruiting student athletes who were committed to hard work. Kevin Cheadle and Rickey Black, members of our church, had attended Jewell and had only positive things to say about it. I also had spoken with of one my coworkers who graduated from William Jewell, and she assured me he made a great choice. I was glad to hear such positive things about the school. I had visited the school, but I wanted his decision to be his own.

Jewell was committed to excellence and dedication. It required its athletes not only to perform well on the field and track, but in the classroom as well.

Willie chose to pursue a career in architectural engineering. I could see that William Jewell developed character and physical abilities in its students. I was in agreement with the staff, who believed excellence in competition translated into excellence in life. And all I wanted was the best for him.

Willie was relieved after making his decision to attend William Jewell. He had walked the campus of Jewell and was no longer focusing on high school. He was anticipating the opportunity to play and break the records that were currently displayed in Jewell's trophy case.

Willie was also looking forward to his senior trip to

Cancun. I was a little reluctant when he asked my permission. I'd heard so many stories about young people when they were out of the country. And the stories were not good. But in the long run, I agreed. I also provided the money for the deposit. There was a problem with the deposit, but it was worked out, and now they were ready to go. Willie had a part-time job and a bank account. He was good at saving money, but he would not have been pleased unless I contributed to his spending money.

Willie and Terrence Roland were like brothers, and they were roommates on the trip. Terrence was a track team member and had come from Westport High. He was a great addition to Hickman Mills boys track; he had set numerous records. He and Willie spent a lot of time together.

Willie was shy in some areas, and it was Terrence who played a part in his transition to popularity. I couldn't have selected a better friend for Willie. He was a genuine and respectable young man. From the first day they met, they had each other's back.

The trip to Cancun would not only be Willie's first trip out of the country, it would also be his first time in an airplane. I am sure there are things that took place on that trip that I will never hear about, but I trusted them, and that was all that mattered.

One day while on the trip, he phoned home and was unable to reach me. So he reached out to his cousin

Aaron, who was home when he called. He had lost his senior class ring while parasailing. We had gone all out for his ring, including diamonds. He deserved it, and was not a child who asked for much. So, when I could do something special for him, I found it easy to deliver. When he returned home, I reassured him we would replace it.

Willie enjoyed Cancun for that week, and I looked forward to his return. I rode with Ann, Terrence's mom, to pick them up from the airport. She too was a single mother. On the way home from the airport, we listened to Terrence and Willie as they chuckled as if they had a secret. Terrence had taken a movie camera on the trip, and I wanted to see that footage. I so wanted to hear what it was like in Cancun, what Willie did and with whom.

He had not been on Kansas City soil long when he shared an incident about a young guy who had died on the trip. It was eerie. I could think only about that mother who sent her son off on a senior trip only to have him never return home. I thought about Willie. What would I do had it been my son?

I could not stop thinking about that mother. So many sad thoughts entered my mind. I felt so sad in that moment, just thinking of this mother I never met. Her son was not a student from Hickman, but a student just the same. The thought of the loss hurt me to the core. It took me a while to be able to change my focus.

Once Willie and I arrived home, his sisters greeted him as if he had been off to war. Of course, he brought his sisters some beautiful souvenirs. As I watched him pulling gifts out of his suitcase, all I could think about was the fact that while he was vacationing, he was thinking about his family. There was one gift that he was unable to find after sorting through the souvenirs, which was the gift for his Grandma Mary. He had purchased her a muumuu, an easy-to-pull-on, comfortable dress with side seam pockets, gathers, deep arm holes, and loose, non-constricting sleeves made of soft, machine-washable polyester and worn as a house dress. Grandma Mary wore muumuus daily, and Willie had not forgotten her on his senior trip.

Willie's dad was always on his mind, even in Cancun. Although he did not see him often, there was a souvenir for him. Willie purchased a beautiful stone sculpture of Jesus Christ for his dad. I still have this sculpture. Willie never gave up on anything, especially his dad. He tried endlessly to connect with him to present him with the gift. It never came to pass.

CHAPTER 7

*The ultimate measure of a man is not where he stands
in moments of comfort, but where he stands at times of
challenge and controversy.
~ Martin Luther King Jr.,*

*Father to the fatherless, defender of widows — this is
God, whose dwelling is holy. ~ Psalm 68:5
New Living Translation (NLT)*

Chapter 7

Willie's senior year had been a roller coaster, and little by little it had come to a close. It was August, and in a matter of days he would be leaving to begin conditioning to play college football. Prior to him leaving, we were bumping heads a lot. If I said yes, he said no, and if I said up, he said down. We had been in disagreements before, but not like this. There would be days when our voices would escalate back and forth in anger. I never considered he was going through something. I could only see that he was being disrespectful, but there was a deeper issue.

Willie was about to go off to school and had not had any time or contact with his dad. I did not realize how heavy that weighed within him. Although he had accomplished so much, there was still a void. We were swinging from one emotional state to another. Willie wanted his father in his life and had also invited his dad to see him off to college, but once again his father was unable to be there. Significant male role models come in many different forms: immediate family, friends, school teachers, and coaches. Role models have a major impact on an impressionable youngster. Willie enjoyed the surrogate fathers in his life, but he wanted his dad. And he did not hold his tongue concerning his wish for me and his father to reconcile.

I never discouraged his father from being a constant in his life. I was his father's number-one supporter when it came to being a father. Willie Sr. had been raised by one of the best. I knew the importance of Willie's dad in his life, but his father would have to make that decision.

At the young age of five, two months shy of his sixth birthday, Willie witnessed a domestic dispute between his father and me that could have altered his beliefs about the way a man should treat a woman. But the respect of women had been instilled in him early. Willie held on to that teaching.

This was one of many times he would be traumatized. Yet that particular incident did not keep him from loving his father. He came to know that forgiving people who hurt him or hurt those he loves would help him achieve greater well-being. He knew that forgiving was something that a person does for himself and not for somebody else. He knew forgiving someone was not saying that what they did was okay or excusing the wrong they did, but provided them freedom from what took place.

Willie was affected by the divorce of his father and me like any other five-year old would be. Death comes in many forms. Divorce is a type of death, and my son felt the pain of our divorce and growing up without a father in the home. He was scarred emotionally, and he confronted the repercussion of divorce often, but he was not bound by the hurt. As young as he was, he never gave up.

I reiterated time and time again to his father not to let the divorce keep him from being a father to his son. You would think that would go without saying. But he allowed people to get inside his head, and he allowed his mistake and pride to keep him from a relationship not only with Willie but also with his daughters. Children grow up quickly, and those special times cannot be revisited afterward. Priorities may mean less money in the bank account, but some experiences are priceless.

There were times when Willie would act out at school, hoping his father would come. He would become disruptive and rebellious, which was very similar to my behavior when I was an adolescent.

I remember one time Willie had taken it upon himself to disregard his teacher's instructions and the consequence for his action was to have him sit in an isolated part of the playground by himself during recess. I can only imagine Willie sitting for as long as he could as he watched the other children play when he decided he could not take anymore. He picked himself up off the playground and left the area where he was instructed to sit. It was obvious no one was paying any attention to him so he took it a step further and left school grounds. It was not until recess came to an end that the teacher realized Willie was gone.

Willie was a thinker and knowing my son he thought carefully about his next move. In that moment of solitude on the playground he devised a plan and enforced it. Willie may have been in the second grade, but he was not the average young man. Remember he took it upon himself to be the man of the house. It was nothing to think up a plan when he believed he was not being treated fairly. He felt he had been dealt a bad hand. His plan was not a safe one. There is nothing worse than a child aimlessly walking without a guardian. He felt his hands had been tied unfairly and wanted justice. In his well thought out orchestrated plan he knew his destination and felt no reason to inform those who had left him unattended while they went about their way.

I was working in the City Clerk's office at the time; across town on the 25th floor of City Hall. I was in fact all the way downtown when I received a call from the school informing me that Willie was missing and they had no idea when he had left or where he was. I do not know how long it took the staff before they conjured the nerve to call me to inform me of my son's whereabouts or the lack thereof. I had to be realistic. I was many miles from where he was last seen and I had no idea where he was and had no idea where to start looking. Nor did I know what had brought on his decision to run away from the school. All I knew was my son was missing and I needed to remain as calm as I could. That is something that would come natural to me in situation of this magnitude. I was able to remain calm. I asked what happened and she explained how he was being punished and was told to sit on the side of the building during the recess period. I was disappointed and could not understand how although he was being punished no one was keeping an eye on him. The school told me not to worry, that they would notify me as soon as they found him. Not worry was easier said then done. Who was to say they would find him?

The only thing I could do was pray; which was the best thing I could do being so far from the school. My hands were tied. It was prayer that gave me peace and kept me from running out the door. I did not have a cell phone at the time and me leaving and running out the door 25 floors down, catching one bus and then transferring to another bus would not be the smartest thing to do. Had they found him or had something else occurred there would be no way to reach me.

So once I finished praying I was led to call Grandma Mary who lived in midtown. I knew she would be home. She was a housewife and at this time of day she would still be in her muumuu in front of the TV or on the front porch reading the paper and holding a conversation with her neighbor, Mrs. Hobbie. My grandmother lived in a neighborhood where everyone knew everybody. It was one of those neighborhoods where if you did something the neighbor was allowed to chastise you and when you got home you would get spanked as well. As quickly and as clearly as I could, I shared the information about what had taken place at school, she interrupted me and said, "I know, he is here, and he said he does not want to go back and he does not have to." I was relieved that he was okay and even more at ease because he had a safe haven. He had gone to a place that was safe and out of harm's way and received the attention he didn't believe he was receiving at school. My grandmother told me she had prepared him something to eat and he was fine. She gave the phone to him and all I had to say was "I love you" and told him I would see him later.

Of course, he had scared the living daylights out of me and I don't know what I would have done had he gone missing too much longer. But this was not the time to scold him, especially over the phone. Grandma Mary had him and that is all that mattered. She knew what to say and how to handle the situation at hand. Grandma Mary was what the Black community would refer to as "big momma," old school, so there was no doubt he would be dealt with. For now I was pleased that he was OK.

My prayers had been answered and I was content and thankful for the moment. Although Willie never should have left school grounds I was grateful he had a Grandma Mary, someone he knew and trusted to look after him.

Grandma Mary was the matriarch of the family, not a title someone gave her, but a role she took on. Even when we were wrong she was able to correct us and still show us our worth. Willie knew he was wrong for leaving, but was aware he had been left unattended.

I would like to think it was in those times Willie was coming into his own, realizing who he was and whose he was. When I got him home we talked about it and although things turned out well I wanted to be certain he understood running away solved nothing because he would be returning to school.

I had to help him through those trying times. It was not as if something was wrong with Willie. His behavior was in response to what had happened to him.

A father's role is crucial in helping to establish the healthy development of a child. Willie was born into this world with the DNA from both his dad and me.

It only made sense that we both would be accountable. I was the custodial parent who assumed the responsibility of providing all the essential needs for him. But there was nothing I could do to influence his dad to spend time with him. I would tell him all the time that it was not about the money, even though I could use it. It was more important that he spend time with his kids, especially Willie.

Rachelle Law

CHAPTER 8

I have learned over the years that when one's mind is made up, this diminishes fear.
~ Rosa Parks

"For God hath not given us the spirit of fear; but of power, and of love, and of a sound mind."
~ 2 Timothy 1:7
King James Version (KJV)

Chapter 8

Willie received a dual scholarship — academic and athletic — to William Jewell College. It was September, and the fall semester was underway. Willie was a student athlete seeking a degree in architectural engineering. He was an incredible athlete, and education was important to him. As a William Jewell Cardinal, he played the position of wide receiver. He proudly wore number 87, which was the same number he wore at Hickman Mills High. He followed in the footsteps of Edward Coody, a very popular upperclassman that lived in an apartment complex in our neighborhood. Willie, Edward, and Lester Jones had known each other since 1993, when Willie was a sixth-grader at Ervin Junior High School. The three of them were known to spend countless hours playing football. Now, seven years later, Willie was in college on a football scholarship.

Willie was allowed to come home to attend his Aunt Jackie's funeral one weekend. He had only been gone a few weeks, yet he was anxious to return home. Any time with family was a good time. William Jewell College was only about forty-five minutes away. His sisters and cousins were excited to see Willie. They enjoyed the opportunity to revisit the time Willie flipped off his Aunt Jackie. Willie didn't recall the moment, but that did not keep his first cousins Aaron and Brittany, Jackie's only daughter; Ebony and his sisters from talking about what had happened many years before.

Willie sat next to me at Aunt Jackie's home-going celebration. He did not say much. He cried quietly. Willie loved his Aunt Jackie. I thought about this throughout the service, as trails of tears rolled down his face. Aunt Jackie never married Ebony's dad, Steve, but regardless of their differences, they remained friends and raised Ebony together. While sharing in the repast after the burial, Steve commented on how much Willie looked like his nephew, who had died recently from injuries sustained in a car accident. Steve's comment was unsettling to me. For whatever reason, it struck a chord deep in my soul. I found myself at a loss for words.

The hour grew late, and it was time to drive Willie back to Jewell. He wanted to stay home longer, but I insisted he return. I overlooked the circumstances; I never stopped to consider what he was going through emotionally. My concentration was getting him back to school so he didn't get behind in his studies. Sometimes I was so busy trying to do the right thing; I would do the wrong thing. Perhaps had I listened to his request, we never would have had the argument—not just any argument, but the biggest argument we ever had with each other.

As we traveled down the highway, Willie mentioned his desire to attend the upcoming homecoming game: Ruskin High School vs. Hickman Mills. It was only natural that Willie wanted to attend, this being his first year as alum. Ashley was up for homecoming queen, and of course Willie would be her escort. I had no objections to him returning for homecoming until the unsettling comment from Steve. I could not help but think it was a forewarning. I now waited for the other shoe to drop.

Finally, we arrived back at William Jewell campus after what seemed like a short ride. I told Willie that he couldn't come home for homecoming. And I was adamant. As we entered the football dorm Willie continued to plead his case. Our voices became loud. Regardless of what I said, he stood his ground and mumbled, "Oh, yes I am." He was determined to do what he wanted to do. And I was just as stubborn as he was. Where do you think he got it from? There is a stubborn streak that runs as long as the day is long in our family.

There was no time for this unending argument. I spoke my peace, and that was that. I had nothing to base my decision on other than the fear that had a grip on me. Everyone had school the next day. Rhonda, my brother's wife and a teacher in the school district, was driving. The waiting area was full of tension. Willie gave me a half-hearted hug, shrugged his shoulders, and walked away.

I felt Michele and Ashley's cold stares burning into me when my back was turned. *I had made my decision, and there was no going back on it now.* Even though I didn't have a leg to stand on, I knew they were right. As the mother, I had handled the situation poorly.

The ride home took forty-five minutes to an hour, but it seemed to last for hours. No one, which included Rhonda, his cousins, and his sisters, said a word. The only sound I could hear were the tires rolling along on the pavement. I felt all alone in a car full of people. My rationale was if Willie stayed at school, everything would be okay. Geography had nothing to do with what was preordained.

We had been riding for twenty-five minutes and still not a word. I knew I needed to make it right as soon as I got home. I needed to apologize. If only I could convince Rhonda to drive faster without causing an accident, I would have. I wanted to get home to call Willie and make things right between us.

We reached our exit. We were a block away. I barely got in the front door when Ashley reached for the phone. She had the most disappointing look on her face when she said, "You need to call him." She placed the phone in my hand and walked away. My heart sank, but she was right. I dialed his number and prayed he would answer. The phone rang and he picked up. "Hello."

"I was wrong and I am sorry!" I said. "I was out of order. Will you forgive me?" I continued to tell him how sorry I was for being such a jerk. My heart was hurting, and as we talked, I prayed he would understand my behavior. He did not hesitate when he said, "I forgive you, Momma." Those words were golden. It was late when we said good-bye. I hung up the phone, and I *cried*.

CHAPTER 9

*The weak can never forgive. Forgiveness is the attribute
of the strong.
~ Mahatma Gandhi*

*But if you refuse to forgive others, your Father will not
forgive your sins. ~ Matthew 6:15
New Living Translation (NLT)*

Chapter 9

After a very trying week, I felt like I could finally take a breath. I worked in the marketing department of a major league baseball team. As the event planner for a corporate sponsorship event, I needed to knock it out of the park. It was homecoming weekend, and I was anticipating Willie playing in his first game at Jewell.

I received unexpected call midweek from Willie. I picked up the receiver. "Hello, this is Rachelle."

The voice on the other end said, "Hey, Momma." That low voice was normal, but there was urgency in it, which concerned me.

I asked, "How are you doing? What's up?"

He said, "I forgive Daddy." His statement took me aback. Willie continued to talk, "I forgive Daddy for not coming to my games." I didn't interrupt him. I could tell how much he wanted to get it off his chest. He paused.

I asked, "Are you okay?" I wished I could be there with him. If only to wrap my arms around him to tell him I understood.

He said, "Yes, I'm okay." I wondered if he'd tried to call his dad and was unsuccessful. "I'm headed to football practice. I'll talk to you later."

I told him how much I loved him, and he said, "I love you too. Bye."

I ended the call but the conversation continued playing in my mind. *What could have happened during his day that triggered him to call and share with me?* Don't get me wrong; he had shared things before, but this was *big*. My thoughts must have been written all over my face, because Diana asked, "Who was that?" I shared the conversation with her.

Diana then gave me a CD, *Open My Heart* by Yolanda Adams. I enjoyed that CD, but there was a track that spoke to my heart: *Fragile Heart*. I am forever grateful for the gift I received at an unexpected time. Walter Savage Landor wrote, "Music is God's gift to man, the only art of Heaven given to earth, the only art of earth we take to Heaven." The lyrics of that song spoke directly to what I was feeling.

After working so hard, it felt good to be home. Michele made it in from Maryville, Missouri. Ashley was in her bedroom, putting on her homecoming gown. As soon as Willie received clearance from his coach, Michele would head to Liberty to pick him up. The phone rang, and Willie was on the other end of the line. I was excited. I was yelling in the background as Michele spoke with him. It had been only four days before that the homecoming visit was not up for discussion. I was at ease and ready to see Willie escort his sister at halftime.

This was Ashley's senior year. She was known as Clarence's little sister as she walked the halls of Hickman Mills High. Not only was she up for homecoming queen, but she was also in the running for valedictorian. She had been selected to participate in the annual Delta Sigma Theta Cotillion, a youth scholarship program cosponsored by the alumnae chapter of the sorority and the Delta Economic and Educational Development Foundation.

My children had their disagreements as siblings, but their love was so much stronger. Willie was not only their brother; he was the core of our family. He was the man of the house. Yes, that is a lot of responsibility to put on the shoulders of a young man, but he carried the load. I was so proud of him. He overcame so much—being falsely arrested for trespassing and being cut from the basketball team his senior year. As the saying goes, what doesn't kill you makes you stronger. Only those who persevere know how far they can go.

Rachelle Law

CHAPTER 10

Worrying is like a rocking chair, it gives you something to do, but it gets you nowhere.
Glenn Turner

Can you get the attention of the clouds, and commission a shower of rain? ~ Job 38:34
The Message (MSG)

Chapter 10

Michele took my car and headed out to pick up her "Wilby," as she had called him since he was younger.

A cluster of clouds blocked the sun. Surely it was not about to rain. I could hear the drums in the distance. The flag girls appeared and marched in sync with the beat of the drums. I could see a couple of class floats. *Where is Ashley?* That's when a convertible appeared. It was Ashley, hesitantly waving as the onlookers called her name. She was not the Miss America type. I was doing the Miss America wave, and she laughed at the sight. "Here she comes," said my mom, with the biggest grin on her face. A typical grandmother, she was as proud as she could be.

Laughing at Ashley, I overlooked the storm clouds that had moved in closer. And she was so embarrassed for how we were acting. Too bad we did not share in the embarrassment she felt. My mother and I continued to scream and holler. I could not help but continue to tell her how beautiful she was. Ashley was always content being in the background, but that night she shined.

Ashley was riding with her calculus teacher, Mrs. Bynum. Mrs. Bynum was one of the best teachers at Hickman and Ashley's favorite. Later Ashley recalled how Mrs. Bynum glanced at the sky and said, "The heavens are going to open up."

Ashley was certain she would not win. But it didn't matter. She accepted the nomination for what it was: a nomination. She had been nominated because she was a senior athlete. Now, Monique—Money is what I called her—was someone who anticipated winning. She was gorgeous and very popular. Monique and Ashley had become good friends. Monique had one sibling, a brother. Ashley spent countless hours at Money's, and her parents treated Ashley like family.

The parade was winding down after a good thirty to forty-five minutes, the amount of time it took to travel one way to Jewell. I stopped watching the parade and began to look through the crowd for Michele and Willie. I knew realistically they should still be on the road.

The weather was making me anxious. The clouds

were coming in from the northeast, where Michele and Willie were. I began to second-guess myself. *Maybe I should have driven to get him. Maybe I should have stuck to my guns and not allowed him to come home. Could it be something is going to happen?* I was certain they had run into the storm, and I whispered a prayer. Then I nudged my mom, and we headed toward the football stadium. We found a fairly good parking spot, not too far from the stadium but close enough to the exit, so we would not be caught in the after-game traffic.

There were so many familiar faces there and so much excitement in the air. I was so looking forward to the halftime celebration. My mom and I found a seat at the very top of the bleachers, because I wanted to stand, without being told to sit down. The stands began to fill up quickly. I stood up and peered across the parking lot. There was no sight of Michele and Willie. Again I whispered a prayer.

We sat observing the crowd of people, and I pointed out different people to my mom. A large crowd had gathered in the lot behind us. I did not know what was going on, but I intended to find out. I strained my eyes like they were binoculars. I zoomed in, and just as I tightened my view, I heard the sound of someone coming up the bleachers. I did not turn around, thinking I might miss something. I just turned my head quickly. It was Michele, extending her legs as she skipped every other bleacher. She exclaimed how she had to leave Willie and added,

"Everyone is so happy to see him." Willie was the center of attention, the focal point of the crowd.

Michele had waited in the parking lot while Willie changed into his suit—the suit he had worn to his senior prom, the blue pinstripe suit his dad had taken him to purchase. Once he had changed, they had headed across the grass and toward the bleachers. The crowd was so large, I couldn't see him. There were so many people; I could not count them all.

The football players had completed their pregame warm-up and had gone inside. Some time later, the cheerleaders began to line up for the entrance of the team. The game was about to start. Willie was in the parking lot talking with Mr. and Mrs. Thomas, Monique's parents. Willie thought highly of Mr. Thomas. Unknown to us, Mrs. Thomas had been diagnosed with breast cancer. I did not get the opportunity to talk with them that evening, but spoke with them a few days later. Once Willie left the Thomas', he headed our way. He was so handsome, and he had buffed up since he had been away. He was now 210 pounds and in great physical shape—not an ounce of fat.

Finally, he stood on the bleachers with us. Willie gave Grandma Ernestine a kiss on the cheek, wrapped his arm around her, and hugged her tight. He did not have to say a word; his presence and smile said it all. Last, but not least, I received a hug. I was so glad he was home.

I also was thankful he had arrived safely. I leaned over and asked Michele, "How was the ride?" She said the clouds were heavy, but she had no problem driving. She also took time to explain how there wasn't a soul in the dorm waiting area, but as soon as Willie came out, his teammates and dorm buddies came out of the woodwork. She said she stood back in silence, in awe of what she witnessed.

What had taken place only minutes before in the parking lot was a replay. His college teammates had heard he was going to his alma mater's homecoming to escort his sister and had come to give him a hard time. They joked and laughed. As the fellowship ended, they told Willie they would see him in the morning. Michele recalled that watching him with his teammates was priceless.

CHAPTER 11

I am prepared for the worst, but hope for the best.
~ Benjamin Disraeli

Do your best, prepare for the worst – then trust GOD to bring victory.~ Proverbs 21:31
The Message (MSG)

Chapter 11

The weather continued to shift, and not for the better. The winds became stronger as the clouds grew darker. The second quarter was coming to an end. Ashley was down on the sideline, peering over her left shoulder. She gave Willie the eye, and then beckoned him to the field. As Willie walked toward Ashley at the bottom of the bleachers, there was an announcement overhead. With the PA system crackling, the announcer said, "Due to inclement weather, the game will be postponed and played tomorrow."

"Oh no," I said. It was especially disappointing for Ashley. She had been looking forward to that moment. Willie was due back in Liberty the following morning.

Willie spun around and headed back up the

bleachers with Ashley right behind him. There would be no pictures taken, no winner proclaimed, and no celebration of another Hickman win. Grandma Ernestine pulled out her Kodak Instamatic camera and without warning there was a quick flash. A picture is worth a thousand words.

Excited to spend time with old friends, Michele's friends suggested seeing a movie. Normally I would have insisted we all go to the house and enjoy each other's company, but they all had plans of their own. Who was I to stand in the way? We stood at the top of the bleachers, and the rain began to come down in sheets. I could barely see my hands in front of my face. As quickly as Willie had come on the scene, he left. I was not worried. I knew he knew how to take care of himself.

We all took off running, including my mom. We ran fast down the slippery bleachers. We ran through the parking lot as my mom held the umbrella over Ashley's head. And we arrived at the car soaking wet.

My mom got in her car, and Ashley and I got in ours. We sat in the car slightly cold as we peered out the windshield in hopes we would see Willie. The windows were beginning to fog up as the rain continued to beat against the windows. We laughed at the rain, but that same rain would not be considered so funny later.

The crowd began to diminish. We decided to leave and trust that Willie had jumped in the car with one of his classmates. We headed to my brother Bobby's house, no more than a couple of miles from the stadium. When we arrived, we rushed the front door. We were wet and laughing hysterically. We gathered in the breakfast area wet and without a change of clothes. Rhonda asked, "Where are Michele and Willie?" Before we could answer, we heard a car pull into the driveway. I rushed to the front door, peeked out the window, and saw a large, white car I did not recognize. The car door opened, and it was Willie. He was not alone. Darshaun was with him. Darshaun attended our church, and Willie and Darshaun shared the same birth date on different years. Darshaun spent many hours with him prior to leaving for college. The car belonged to Kiyanna's family. Kiyanna, Willie's girlfriend, had been sitting with us at the top of the bleachers. It made sense that he would be with her. He'd learned early to look after the women in his life.

I was surprised to see Darshaun, because I hadn't seen him at the football game. They stood before me even more saturated than we were. I told Willie to take off his suit, which he did. Piece by piece, I carefully laid it on top of the washer in the laundry room, just adjacent to the kitchen. Fortunately, Willie had a change of clothes. He and Kiyanna had planned to meet up later in the evening.

Shortly after Willie's entrance, other friends and

family members arrived. Any other time we would have been at home. I'm not sure how people knew we would be at Bobby's. Rhonda ordered one of Willie's favorite pizzas. Willie, Darshaun, and Ashley went downstairs to visit. The other guests followed. Willie made a phone call to William White, a very close friend who didn't come by because of the weather.

The house was full of life, like during the holidays. Multiple conversations were taking place in every room. The pizza arrived just in time. We were all pretty hungry, as we hadn't eaten prior to the parade or at the game. Willie was the first one to respond to the food call. He was upstairs before the pizza delivery person could get out of the driveway. He stood in the kitchen preparing his plate chewing and laughing at the same time. Rhonda asked, "Are you going to tell anyone else to come and get some pizza?" Willie's response was more laughter.

Ashley and I prepared ourselves to go back out into the rain. When we stepped outside, the once heavy rain had turned into a slight drizzle. I was the designated driver to take Ashley to the dance. Grandma Ernestine had kept Ashley covered with her umbrella, so she was okay to go to the dance without any further preparation. She hated to leave her brother, and she looked over at me and smiled reluctantly.

Upon my return from dropping off Ashley, the guys

decided to take Darshaun home to get some dry clothes. The plan was to go to the dance and then to the skating rink where Kiyanna worked. Willie stood there in a white FUBU shirt that Kiyanna had purchased for him. Kiyanna was a year behind Willie and attended Grandview High school. She was scheduled to graduate in 2001, the same year as Ashley.

I put my hand on Willie's chest and told him how nice he looked. I had barely had time to catch my breath from taking Ashley to the school. Everything was happening so fast, I did not take the time to ask who was driving. That was part of my normal routine when he left the house. "Who's driving? Be careful. Remember whose you are and who you are." I failed to say anything. I assumed Terrence was driving, as he usually did. I was not concerned. The guys were responsible. I gave Willie a hug. He squeezed me tight. Everyone said their good-byes, and they left.

Not long after the guys left the house, Aaron yelled from upstairs at the top of his voice, "An accident!"

CHAPTER 12

"The Lord is my Shepherd, I shall not want..."
~ Psalm 23

Chapter 12

Before Aaron could finish his sentence, I moved robotically to the front door, out the door, and across the vacant lot next to my brother's house. While rushing across the vacant lot, I crossed paths with Mike Hill. At the time, I was unaware he was the driver of the vehicle involved in the accident. I didn't stop to ask him any questions. He appeared to be fine. But his presence puzzled me; he had come out of nowhere.

I continued to walk to the end of the lot over to Overhill Street, the block behind my brother's home. The car was facing north and south on a block that ran east and west. There was a large dent on the driver's side. As I came upon the wreckage I screamed, "Somebody call 911."

I could see Willie. He was sitting directly behind the

driver's seat. I thought he was unconscious. I kissed his forehead and whispered, "I love you." Willie opened his eyes and said, "I love you too." I gave myself permission to exhale. I was scared.

I could see Willie looking at me. I was familiar with that look. The look a child gives their parent when they are seeking comfort. I immediately gave him the comfort he needed. I managed to muster the words, "It's going to be all right." Then I prayed God would give me the comfort I needed.

I kicked into a nurse role and asked Willie where he was hurting. He pointed to his side. I tried to make him as comfortable as possible. I encouraged him to be still. I didn't want him to move. I knew that moving could turn a minor injury into a serious one. There was blood on his shirt—enough blood to cause concern. I couldn't tell where the blood came from. Was it from Willie or Darshaun?

Darshaun was sitting in the back seat on Willie's right side. He was unconscious. I grabbed Darshaun's wrist to check his pulse. I remember thanking God he had a pulse. Matt, a.k.a. Big T, also sat in the back seat to the right of Darshaun. T appeared to be disoriented and repeatedly asked about C-Dub. Terrence was the passenger in the front seat. He got out of the car and stood in the middle of the street, never making eye contact with anyone. He was staring off in the distance as if he were in a trance. Terrence was like the brother Willie never had but always wanted. My eyes were on the guys, but I could hear the voices of onlookers approaching the scene of the accident.

The crash must have been extremely loud. The streets were quickly filling with onlookers from every direction. I don't recall hearing the impact. I only remember Aaron's voice echoing in my ears, "Accident on Bannister."

William Brown, a neighbor, was within arm's reach and offered me his cell phone. I knew I needed to call Monique, Darshaun's mom, and let her know what was happening. I dialed Monique's number as if it were on speed dial. I told her I was sure they would be fine. Maybe a little shook up, yet fine. That was so far from the truth. I didn't know the severity of the injuries. As soon as I hung up, I phoned Willa Robinson, coordinator of the women's ministry at my church. I asked that she start a prayer chain so as many people as possible would be praying for the boys.

Willie was still in the car but was struggling to get out. Aunt Rhonda and I encouraged him to remain still, but he was anxious to get out of the car. I was still in the dark concerning the extent of his injuries. I noticed the driver of the other vehicle was no longer on the scene, but I didn't look for him. His truck was at the top of the hill on the corner of Bannister and Manchester.

Much time had passed, and there was still no sight of an emergency team. One neighbor thought the emergency team was uncertain of the location, which was not something I wanted to hear. There was a fire station a few blocks west. What was happening? Surely the emergency responders from that station were familiar with Bannister Road.

Finally, the emergency team arrived. But the EMT chose to respond to Willie and Darshaun last. Eventually they pulled Darshaun out the back window. It was then they pronounced him dead. *What? No, this could not be happening. Darshaun is dead?* For a moment I stood in disbelief and immediately realized that if I heard it, so did Willie. I know he had heard, because he immediately became extremely anxious to get out of the car.

Willie ended up lying on the wet ground with his foot still trapped in the car seat. I lay in the street with my only son and began to recite Psalm 23 with him. "The Lord is my Shepherd, I shall not want." Willie recited it with me. The only thing I wanted from the Lord was my son to be all right. Willie continued to recite Psalm 23: "He maketh me lie down..." He made Willie lie down. I knew then it was not about me.

It was then I thought back to that conversation on my grandmother's porch. I wondered, *What if?* What if I had stuck to my guns and forbidden him to attend homecoming, forbidden him to leave campus.

But I didn't stay in that place for long. I knew in my heart that I was not sovereign and was not the one in control. This was bigger than me. This was not about me. It was about God and His will. I began to say, "Jesus," repeatedly as I looked over the scene of the accident, expecting a miracle.

As Willie continued to recite the Scripture, I went blank. I could not recall one word. A psalm I knew by memory had become unfamiliar. A psalm of affirmation was examining my faith. "Yea, though I walk through the valley of the shadow of death, I will fear no evil." Could I trust God? Could I trust Him in this shadow of death? I began to declare this was not it. This was not the shadow of my son's death. It was the grace of God that kept me from falling apart. I held on to my faith. *Not my son.* He was a believer and shared it willingly, so surely the Lord had other plans for him.

CHAPTER 13

*Action speaks louder than words but not nearly as
often.
~ Mark Twain*

*"He will answer them, 'I'm telling the solemn truth:
Whenever you failed to do one of these things to
someone who was being overlooked or ignored, that was
me – you failed to do it to me.' ~ Matthew 24:45
The Message (MSG)*

Chapter 13

Willie was still lying in the street. "Help my son!" I cried out. A police officer began to ask questions. I wanted to do whatever was necessary to get my son the medical care he desperately needed. I answered questions over and over again. The focus was on whether or not they had been drinking. The boys were not under the influence. This sort of questioning was stereotypical.

One by one I provided the names, numbers, and addresses to the best of my ability. I pointed in the direction of my brother's home and told the officer they had just left my brother's home. But the officer's perception was his reality. He was not hearing anything I said, because he insisted on asking me the same questions over and over again. Once the officer was through interrogating me, I walked back to the car. Terrence was still standing in the street in disbelief and refused to lie down on the stretcher. Matt did not want to get in the ambulance either. They were concerned about Clarence who was still not getting medical attention.

I noticed my mother was standing nearby. I lashed out and told her to go inside. I had to be out of my mind; I raised my voice at my mom. It was not what I said, but how I said it. The accident was getting the best of me. I could not excuse what I did. I could only apologize. I then asked Mom to go to the house to get my insurance card. I never saw her move so fast. She returned, insurance card in hand. Maybe they needed to know if he was insured, but really they were making excuses for treatments my son was receiving—or should I say not receiving. But even being without insurance should not justify a lack of treatment.

Once I had the insurance card in my hand, I put it in the face of the emergency team and repeatedly said, "He is insured!" Why was he not being taken to the hospital? Everyone else was being taken to the hospital. It was obvious Willie was in critical condition; he took the greatest impact. Darshaun had been pronounced dead, but they were dragging their feet. Did another young kid have to die before they would do something?

As I tried to justify what was being done or not being done, a police officer led me to a car and asked the same questions asked by the other officer. I could not believe how the whole ordeal was being handled. Among other emotions, I was highly irritated. I was going to be sure to make my concerns heard once we got this accident behind us. But first things first; I wanted to help as much as I could so my son could receive the attention he needed. So I cooperated and did whatever was asked of me. If I had to, I would answer the same questions a hundred times, a thousand times — whatever it took.

After speaking with the officer, I saw Bobby and Rhonda. Willie was finally getting the attention he needed. Rhonda and Bobby kneeled by him and the medical technicians. The driver informed me I would not be able to ride with him in the ambulance. My only question was "Why?" Like so many other questions that night, I did not receive a response.

They placed a neck brace on Willie. When they began to move him, he grabbed a hold of Bobby's leg with all his might. My heart sunk. My son wanted desperately not to leave without me. I could only imagine what was going on in his head as he lay there. I told him to let go so he could be placed in the ambulance. "Willie," I said. "Allow them to do their job. I will be right behind you. I will be there."

This had to be a dream. I couldn't believe another police officer approached me with the same questions. I was growing more tired and frustrated by the minute. I slowly turned around, looked directly in the face of the police officer, and waited for him to continue the same line of questioning that had been a theme all night. When I was through with the rerun, "were they drinking?" I looked and no longer saw Willie with my brother.

I ran over to Bobby. "Where is he?" Bobby pointed to an ambulance that was unattended. Yes, my son had head trauma and had been placed in an ambulance and left unattended. The emergency team literally set him off to the side to die. But he would not die on the street. I moved swiftly toward the ambulance and looked helplessly into the window. I could not get in. I tried.

Was there anyone listening to me or my family? Could anyone feel our pain? My eyes filled with tears, but I would not cry; it would all work out. I began approaching medical people to ask why he was being left to die. I requested permission to ride in the ambulance and was rejected.

I remember standing in the middle of Bannister and looking east, asking God, "Please let this cup pass, but if not your will be done." I could not believe what I said. But I said it. I began to cry to God. "Hear my prayer, Lord!" As incomplete as my prayers were, I asked God as many times as the police had questioned me, "See me through." Perhaps the accident was an attack of the enemy. What I know for sure is, at the name of Jesus, demons flee, and there is power in the name of Jesus. So because of what I know, I had to stand on His name and trust Him and His will.

As I stood there, I knew God was working; I just had not grasped what I was to gain from this. *What God? What?* I tried to gain a lesson and knew that I was trapped in a time warp. I wanted out, as if I were in a dream and I wanted to wake up out of fear of what was going on. My heart was breaking. This was the hardest spiritual battle, and I wanted the war to be over.

CHAPTER 14

A life is not important except in the impact it has on other lives.
~ Jackie Robinson

Be careful for nothing; but in everything by prayer and supplication with thanksgiving let your requests be made known unto God. ~ Philippians 4:6
King James Version (KJV)

Chapter 14

Monique and her husband, Craig, arrived. She was in no condition to identify Darshaun, so Craig did. Monique took off running West on Bannister, and I took off after her. She was a track star in high school, so how I caught up with her, I will never know. She literally ran a quarter of a mile and then stood in the street, screaming and crying. My heart was hurting, and I felt her pain too. I didn't know what to say. What could I say? I still hadn't processed the fact that Darshaun was no longer with us.

I'm not sure how we arrived back at the scene, but when we got there, Willie was gone. *Where is he? Where is my son?* I was very disturbed. How on earth was it I had been on the scene so long? I asked a plethora of questions and no one—not one officer, not one medical technician—bothered to tell me where my son had been taken. I was dumbfounded.

The number of unanswered questions mounted. The night was unreal and frightening. It felt like an Alfred Hitchcock movie.

Before I could open my mouth to ask God, "Where?" I got a call from Michele. She had been at the movies with her girlfriends and gone home after the movie, where she heard Willie had been injured in a car accident. She had immediately called her girlfriends and asked them to turn around to pick her up. The hospital was maybe ten miles from the scene. While waiting for her friends to come back she said, "God, Your will be done."

Darshaun's Aunt Michelle left a message on our answering machine. She had no idea her nephew had been pronounced dead on the scene. Michelle and Maesha, her daughter, had been driving nervously around the city looking for the hospital they assumed Darshaun was in, with a gas tank registering empty. She was clueless her nephew was never taken to a hospital, but transported to the city morgue.

Michelle had no idea that I was still on the scene and had been since about 10:30 p.m. It was approaching midnight. I did not even know where Willie was. The mother of the injured party, I had not been allowed to ride in the ambulance and had been left at the scene of the accident for more than an hour. I was the one answering all the questions. I was the one assisting them at every command, only to be left

125

standing in the middle of the street. And now they were looking for me.

By this time Ashley had phoned Rhonda and Bobby's house to be picked up from the homecoming dance. She had no idea what had taken place. She too had gone home; she had arrived there before Michele and left her shoes in the middle of the floor. The house was quiet and eerie; she knew something was wrong. Ashley also knew nothing would have kept Willie from coming to the dance unless something unexpected had happened.

I'm not sure how she got home. It did not seem important at the time. I also do not know who answered the phone when Ashley called my brother's home; but no one wanted to be the one to deliver the news. After the phone had been passed around the table with no one having the courage to speak with Ashley, she eventually demanded somebody come and get her. Brittany, Ashley's first cousin, and her uncle Rodney agreed to go get her.

CHAPTER 15

While there's life, there's hope.
~ Marcus Tullius Cicero

For you know that when your faith is tested, your
endurance has a chance to grow. ~ James 1:3
New Living Translation (NLT)

Chapter 15

By the time Ashley arrived on the scene, we knew where Willie was. Rhonda had started the van up and had agreed to drive. No one felt that I should be driving. I opened the door of the van, climbed up in the front passenger seat, and off to the hospital we went. Somehow Rhonda was confused about where the hospital was, though she was familiar with the area. It was on the same road she traveled each weekend to shop at one of the biggest malls in the area. We all had taken that route for years. But with all that was going on, she became perplexed and had taken the wrong turn. Rhonda reaffirmed that she would get me there. I had no doubt about that, but I had an uneasy feeling about what and who would be there when we arrived.

I gained a momentary sense of peace. Maybe it was the fresh air blowing on me through the lowered window. There had been so much pandemonium; this was a tranquil pause in the evening. It was the first time since the crash I was able to gather my thoughts and to prepare myself for what lay ahead. Then a dreadful vision of Ashley sitting on the curb appeared in my thoughts. I had been so anxious to get to the hospital; I had jumped in the van and unintentionally left her curbside in a formal gown and tennis shoes.

In a matter of minutes, we arrived at the hospital. Should I ever need immediate attention from a medical team, drive me to the inner city hospital that sits on a hill. Get me to the hospital that has a trauma team that's familiar with accidents of this nature.

As we took the ramp exit and bared left into the emergency room parking lot of the hospital, my heart began to race. Deep in my soul I already knew what I would find on the other side of the automatic doors, which opened up the same way that heaven did that night.

Michele greeted me at the emergency room door. She asked, "How are you doing? The hospital staff tried to contact you." I thought, *Sure they did.* In the past hour, I had gone from a one to a ten after being denied the opportunity to ride in the ambulance and not informed where my son would be taken—not to mention being frightened and anxious as I waited to hear his fate. At that point, I could care less what they tried to do.

As Michele and I walked to the sitting area, we were met by Melanie. Melanie had crossed a similar path a few years back in the loss of her sister and her niece. I welcomed Melanie and Nicole coming out to support us in such a difficult time. She is the daughter of Willa Mae Robinson, whom I had phoned from the scene of the accident requesting prayer.

Knowing that prayer changes things, I whispered a prayer. It was not long before the nurse approached me and requested I go to a private room. Speaking sternly, I said, "I am not going to any room." I may have been new to the state of affairs, but I was not new to the emergency room. I worked as an EKG tech in the emergency room, so I am familiar with the "private room." I was wet, cold, and sitting in a waiting room. A "private room" was not what I wanted to hear.

CHAPTER 16

*The dead cannot cry out for justice. It is a duty of the
living to do so for them.*
~ Lois McMaster Bujold

*Is there not an appointed time to man upon earth? Are
not his days also like the days of a hireling? ~ Job 7:1
King James Version (KJV)*

Chapter 16

As the white coats approached, the words arrived ahead of them. The writing was on the wall. I could almost see them rehearsing the lines in their eyes. I looked straight ahead as one mouthed, "We tried, but he did not make it." Then, in the same breath, "Can we have his eyes?" With my hands hanging down by my side, I began to roll my fingers one by one into a ball to make a fist. "No, you can't have his eyes. You've got to be kidding!" Literally shaking at the knees, I stood there with my fists clenched, desperately wanting to hit something.

I had been to hell and back, and all of a sudden there was urgency. Where was the urgency when Willie was lying in the street? No! You can't have my son's eyes! No! No! No! A thousand times, *no*! Now that there were organs that could be used for someone *else*, the sense of urgency was there.

I walked to the nearby wall and began to beat the wall with all that was within me. I pounded one fist after another into the wall until my muscles grew tired and I could no longer strike it with any significant force. Who cares about my loss? They were on to other lives. The doctor stared as if I were unsure, but there was no indecisiveness. My son would not be a donor. As you read this you may think of me as heartless and cold, but when a patient dies, there's a window of four to six hours to extract the eyes, and the procedure itself takes only twenty to thirty minutes. So there was no need for their heartless insensitive "urgency."

"May I see my son?" I said, as I looked the other way. *What was the hold up?* Willie had been in their charge for at least twenty minutes.

While I waited to be cleared to see Willie, Ashley arrived. She stood there expressionless. A day of celebration had turned into a day of unforgettable sadness.

She asked repeatedly, "Is he dead?" Although I was standing an arm's distance from her, I didn't respond. I had mentally checked out. I couldn't stop the tape recorder of my mind. I replayed the night over in my head. *What happened? Was this for real?* I was devastated. I wanted to die.

This was a first for me, the first time I received the

news of a loved one's death. I had been there for other people. Melanie began to make calls to friends and loved ones to tell them that Willie had died from injuries sustained in a car accident. She managed to contact loved ones without very little help from me.

Finally I was told I could see Willie. Michele, Rhonda, Melanie, Nicole, and I were escorted to the room that held my son's body. It was obvious the delay was not because they were trying to make him presentable. Willie was lying on the table in the center of the room. It was mind-blowing to see him lying on a gurney, lifeless. His left leg was twisted and hanging off the gurney. His blood-stained FUBU shirt was ripped from top to bottom, which left his chest exposed. The tubes and medical equipment were in disarray. There was no denying anything. He was *gone*.

Willie had been pronounced dead at 11:50 p.m.; it was now midnight. Usually, the hospital staff makes the deceased presentable for the family. Not this hospital. Not my son. Not today. Yet they wanted me to donate his eyes. *Did they even care?* From the look of things, I doubt it.

I stood glassy eyed over the gurney in disbelief. So many songs ran through my head. Willie loved to sing and rap. He sang songs with so much passion; like "Meet You at the Crossroad" and "911." I found it hard to concentrate on anything. My mind was racing. I didn't know what to do or how to respond.

I just stood there, wishing he would rise like Lazarus.

My one and only beloved son lay before me at the age of eighteen, dead. *What now?* There was nothing left to do, but I could not walk away. All I wanted was a miracle, but the reality was staring me in my face. Willie was deceased.

I felt no one cared. The thought of me not being there in the last minutes of his life hurt terribly. I couldn't stop looking at his lifeless body. I became angry the more I stood there. Angry at the thought of the care he and his friends received.

My son wasn't air-transported to a hospital, yet he had suffered life-threatening injuries. The perception was that Willie and his friends were joyriding and drinking, but neither of the two was accurate. Willie was home to escort his sister for homecoming, but how would they know; they never bothered to ask. It was difficult to make sense of it all. I had no idea what to do.

As I walked out of the room, I heard footsteps. When I looked up, I realized it was Bobby and Ashley going to view Willie's body. When I returned to the waiting room, Bobby and Ashley were not far behind me. Bobby said, "Willie's gone!"

"What do you mean, Willie's gone?" I asked.

"He's not back there." I could not understand what was taking place.

My nightmare got worse. There was a waiting room full of friends and family who wanted to view his body. Being undone, I demanded to see someone. "What is going on?" I asked the nurse. "We are not invisible. Did it cross your mind that his friends and family would like to view his body? You took longer to inform me of his death than to allow me to view his body."

The nurse said, "He is now property of the state."

I thought, *are you serious? My son is neither a criminal nor a prisoner of the jail system.* "How can you stand there and tell me he is property of the state?" No one could or would explain. I could only shake my head. I stood in the hallway with Ashley, being told she could not see her brother. I could only imagine what may have been going through her head. First I had left her on the curb and then she could not see the remains of her brother's body. While I was seeking answers, Bobby found the morgue and was able to view him.

Having had enough, I turned around, and there was a crowd of people, standing in front of me. Who was there? I couldn't name them one by one. Not that their presence was insignificant. I just couldn't clearly identify everyone. There was one face that did stand out in the crowd. No, it wasn't a member of my family. It was a woman I had looked up to for many years. I admired her walk with God. She was a mighty prayer warrior, Lelar Williams. She was not alone, but it was as if she were.

Lelar, a tall, fair-skinned, beautiful woman of God, stood above the rest. If I wanted prayer, I could count on her praying, not just saying she would pray. Whenever I think of the events at the hospital, I see her face. She has a son, an only son, and if anyone understood, she did. I thank God for her presence that night. If for one minute I had any doubt someone was praying, Lelar was my confirmation someone was praying. People were standing in the gap, praying for my son. God answers prayer according to His Will. He knows the plans He has for us. I know I loved Willie, but God loved him more.

While I sat and ran the night over in my head, Willie's paternal grandmother entered with a friend and her pastor. She rested her head on my lap, and I could smell alcohol on her breath. I rose to my feet, and she slithered off my lap. I was not in the mood for her or the drama.

I wanted to get as far from the hospital as possible. Lisa was in the waiting area and just like that she appeared as my ram in the bush. Lisa and I attended church together. She was like an aunt to my children and was very familiar with the relationship between my ex-mother-in-law and me. She could relate to what I was experiencing, as she had experienced the loss of a very special man in her life, her father.

As she and I were walking to the car, Aunt Kim appeared. She was not really Willie's aunt, but our children had grown up together in the church. Kim had two sons, Mike and Anthony. I could only imagine her thinking of her sons during this time. The news of Willie's death was startling. However, I could tell she was irritated and not by his death, but how the news was delivered. She had barely entered the door when she was told Willie was dead. The news was so unexpected.

When dealing with death, people often don't express their feelings in a positive way. Often they stick their foot in their mouth by saying insensitive things. They think they have to say something when it would be better if they kept their mouth closed.

I was grateful for the support, but I just wanted to go home. I'd had enough of the police department, the medical staff, and everyone who was assigned to help. I was *angry*. My question was not why, but why now. Willie was a freshman in college, ministering to others, volunteering, and making something of himself. I couldn't help but think of the young men in the world who were committing senseless crimes with no remorse. Why not take their life? Take someone that is a menace to society. I know that is a horrible thing to say, but that is what I thought. The menace is someone's son. I know my flesh was talking, but my flesh was reigning.

While waiting in the car for Rhonda to take me home, I sat gazing at the raindrops that rested on the window. I was mad as hell. It was no longer raining or even misting. The storm had passed. It was late. I was mentally and emotionally drained. I wondered, *what now?* Bannister, a street I traveled daily, was now one I dreaded to travel. Only a few hours before, the house had been full of life and family. Now we had one less family member, and the house appeared dark and cold. Rhonda and Bobby had been reluctant for us to go home. I heard her tell him, "They can't go home." But she was right there and did everything to make me and the girls comfortable. That night the girls and I slept at their home.

In the silence, the doorbell rang. I said, "Who on earth could it be?" Bobby answered the door and called me; it was Willie's father. It was uncanny how I had repeatedly asked him to be involved in Willie's life, and it took his death for him to show up. He had no idea what to say. What could he say? Absolutely nothing. He asked, "What can I do? Let me know if you need anything." Willie was no longer there, so what could he say or do?

Hell, I needed him to be a father to his children, but he did not have time. I needed him to spend time with his son, but he didn't have time. Now that Willie was dead, he found time. All I could think was for him to get the hell out of my face. But as he turned away, I thought about what Willie had said to me earlier that week. He had forgiven his father. Regardless of the father he had been, Willie forgave him. And because he could forgive, he had left this earth in peace. That midweek call had been for me. Regardless of the father he wasn't to Willie, I had to forgive him. Willie's father left and it would be a long time before we exchanged words.

I began to think how I would never hear Willie's voice again. I was so afraid of not hearing his voice; I called his dorm room and got his answering machine. I did it again and again. After the fourth call, I stopped.

It was a while before I went to sleep, but I did sleep. Before closing my eyes, I whispered a familiar prayer, "Now I lay me down to sleep..." and asked the Lord to see us through.

CHAPTER 17

With the new day comes new strength and new thoughts.
~ Eleanor Roosevelt

Create in me a clean heart, O God; and renew a right spirit within me. ~ Psalm 51:10
King James Version (KJV)

Chapter 17

It was eight o'clock Saturday morning. This was the first day without my only son. I would try to get through it. Slowly the family came downstairs one by one. No one said anything. No one knew what to say. What do you say? Willie was dead at eighteen.

There was no evidence it had rained the night before. The sun was shining on both sides of the street—a phrase Grandma Mary used when the sun was shining brightly. Now I had to call her and tell her Willie had died.

Calling Grandma Mary was one of the hardest things I've ever had to do. My cousin Tirria answered the phone. I shared the news, and she yelled, "No, Shellie!" (Shellie is my nickname in the family.) When she relayed the news, Grandma Mary immediately fell to her knees. That Monday she had lain to rest her daughter Jackie. Here it was Saturday morning and she was receiving news of her grandson dying from injuries sustained in a car accident. Willie's death had shattered the world as we knew it.

Next I called Willie's coach. The news of Willie's death unquestionably caught the coach off guard. He had been expecting Willie back on campus for the football game. Michele, Ashley, and I were scheduled to head up to Liberty that morning for the first home game to celebrate family weekend. Willie had requested seven tickets, and he told me he did not know why he asked for that many. I instantly thought of the biblical reference in the book of Revelation stating that the number seven is the number of completeness and perfection. Willie had run his race, and he had been perfected.

Breaking bad news to the coach at Jewell and Grandma Mary was not a pleasant task, but delaying the news would have been even worse. I knew it was important to call specific people before the news hit the grapevine.

Although it's hard for those who receive bad news, it is hard telling bad news. It was especially hard sharing the news with Lydia, my girlfriend, and her husband, Kelvin. They had spent countless hours with my children, and Kelvin was one of Willie's basketball coaches. There were times Lydia would literally be reaching for her inhaler because of something Willie said or did.

I was unaware Lydia was home alone when I blurted out, "Willie died last night in a car accident." Lydia began to scream and cry simultaneously. She dropped the phone, and all I could hear was her screaming and crying. "Shellie, no!" She told me how much she loved me and the girls and said she would be over soon.

I could hear the family getting restless as I hung up from Lydia. I wanted to talk with Ann, Terrence's mom. It had been only three months before that Terrence and Willie attended the senior trip to Cancun. When I called, I could tell Ann had not heard that Willie did not survive his injuries. There was a long pause when I told her the news. She said, "I sensed something was going to happen. I cannot explain it." She too had a gut-wrenching feeling about that night.

The family gathered in the kitchen eating area. Willie's suit was still on the washer in the laundry room, adjacent to the kitchen. It was still damp from the rain. I had unconsciously laid it on the washer so meticulously. From where I was sitting in the kitchen, I could look out the kitchen window and see the spot where the accident took place. My brother's house was the last place I wanted to be. I grew tired of replaying the incident over and over again, but I couldn't stop remembering as long as I was in that house, on that block. At least that is what I told myself.

By now I assumed everyone knew we were at Bobby's. Hindsight is 20/20. I sat at the table reflecting on conversations and tidbits leading up to the events. Michele, Ashley, and I shared the dreams we had concerning Willie's death. I recalled the conversation Willie shared with Michele and me about his heavenly mansion. He could not describe it, but he confirmed he saw his mansion. I remembered the nervousness I felt about him coming home.

I was proud of how my girls were carrying themselves. Willie had been the core of our family. Even though they hadn't said much, I was concerned about their vulnerability. I kept them covered in prayer. They were surrounded by many who truly loved them.

The photographs from my mom's Kodak camera were developed. A picture *is* worth a thousand words. The final picture was of Willie and Ashley standing on the top bleacher at the football stadium. There would never be a picture including Willie again. This was it. Looking at the pictures, I thought of the football games. I thought how today Willie would have been playing his first college home game and Hickman Mills would be playing the postponed game.

The William Jewell football team cut their sleeves off

and wore them on their heads, something Willie had initiated in high school. The Hickman Mills vs. Ruskin final score was Hickman 8 and Ruskin 7 — 87 — the number Willie wore in high school and in college. There were very few people in attendance that did not realize the symbolism of the eight-to-seven victory.

After a heartfelt conversation with my brother and sister-in-law, the girls and I went home. I appreciated all they had done, but it was time to go home. The ride home was a somber one. I had no desire for questions or conversation. I wanted to take a shower. I'd finally have a chance to be alone. Someone else could be on duty and take calls. I needed some "me" time, time to process, to cry. My objective was to release the tension that had settled in my bones and my soul after the long night. In the shower, I would let my guard down. The bathroom is where I always had my early-morning quiet time with God.

I entered the bathroom — my throne room — and closed the door behind me. I undressed, removing the clothes I had worn since yesterday. I reached for the shower knobs and turned them on full blast. The bathroom began to fill with steam. I wiped the mirror with my fingertips and I stared at the image in the mirror. Fortunately the mirror did not show how much my heart hurt. I wore a brave front, but inside I was falling apart. Just to think of Willie made me tearful. I made up my mind that I was going to take my shower and go to bed. A part of me died when Willie died. Repeating "Willie is dead" was very difficult. I felt sad and angry.

I tested the water to make sure the temperature was comfortable. The water was hot, so hot the bathroom began to feel like a sauna. I closed the shower curtain. Then I sat on the edge of the toilet seat and removed my socks. I lazily walked to the back of the shower as I rested my right hand on the shower wall. Once inside the shower, I stood in the middle of the tub. The water bounced on my head. I moved in closer and began to allow the water to hit me in the face.

As the water landed on the crown of my head and ran down my face, the tears began to flow. The harder the water hit, the harder I cried. I cried steadily. As I cleaned myself, God cleaned my hurt and pain. He washed me with living water. The shower reminded me of the rain that poured from the sky in sheets. The shower took me back to us running to the car as we ran from the bleachers. The shower allowed me to let go of everything that I had bottled up at the hospital. It gave me peace in the midst of the storm.

Once I stepped out of the shower the retreat ended. The phone was ringing and continued to ring into the night—one call after another, friends, family, and even enemies called to confirm his death.
The phone calls led to traffic. There was Sunday

morning traffic and rush-hour traffic. The Sunday morning traffic is people who are genuinely concerned about your well-being. Sunday morning traffic helps in your new journey without your loved one. Sunday morning traffic washes dishes, prepares meals, and does laundry and whatever else comes to mind. Sunday morning traffic provides mental, emotional, and physical support during the time of bereavement. It leads you to the Word and encourages with prayer.

Rush-hour traffic is people with wrong motives. They come by to eat, make a plate, and leave. They create chaos like paparazzi. They are not concerned with your healing process. They take snapshots and use them as gossip.

Visitors changed from day to day. Kiyanna was an everyday visitor. She sat at the table where Willie's track medals, trophies, and pictures were displayed. I remember him telling me how he could talk to Kiyanna about anything. He was happy and had deep feelings for her. I was happy that he experienced a loving relationship with a special person.

Regardless of your home size, Sunday morning traffic and rush hour traffic will visit. I was thankful for the traffic. I received both, but most importantly, I learned from the traffic. I learned to stay in my lane.

In the days to follow, Ashley became our very own cheerleader. "Happy, happy, happy!" she said while clapping her hands. "Willie would want us to be happy." I thought she had lost her mind. But she was right. Her enthusiasm and gesture brought a smile to Michele's face and mine.

Among the many that came by to express their condolences, were students and faculty from William Jewell College. They packed up Willie's dorm room and delivered his personal items. What a blessing! I had the opportunity to meet the young folks he knew during his tenure at Jewell. Willie spoke of one young man in particular, Tyson. Tyson was a teammate that he had met in training camp that summer at Jewell.

Had I not been so prideful, I could have met Tyson prior to Willie's death. One weekend Willie had called and asked permission to bring someone home. Our place was small. *Where would he sleep?* It was a lame excuse, and it never should have stopped us from having guests.

Tyson was standing outside our apartment in tears, and he asked, "Was Clarence saved?"

I stepped back, looked into Tyson's eyes, and said, "Yes! Willie was saved." I thought *how many young men would be able to share their concern for a friend's soul? What a fine man.* Sometimes we miss our blessings because we think it is always about us.

Well, guess what. *It's not!* Tyson pulled himself together, and we went inside.

CHAPTER 18

The timing of death, like the ending of a story, gives a changed meaning to what preceded it.
~ Mary Catherine Bateson

Wherefore, my beloved brethren, let every man be swift to hear, slow to speak, slow to wrath: ~ James 1:19 King James Version (KJV)

Chapter 18

After Willie's death, I found myself overwhelmed with tasks, dealing with the death certificate, financial accounts, tax returns, and funeral arrangements. Normally I am the event planner for the family, and I believe the family thought I knew what to do when Willie died.

Planning Willie's funeral was very emotional. My intention was to have a service that would help in the grieving process. I wanted to make certain his dad and grandmother was included in the planning process. Willie would have wanted it that way. I phoned his dad to provide the necessary information. I was estranged from his paternal grandmother, so I could have easily left her out of the decision making. She had not been involved in his life. Unfortunately, she took every opportunity to create friction during the planning stages as well as in the grieving process. That's not something you'd expect from a woman who had lost a child of her own.

I was thankful for my girls and my mom. During the casket selection, we were able to laugh and smile while making necessary arrangements for Willie's going home celebration. I could not see any reason to have more than one family car for the funeral. As I told the coordinator my decision, Willie's grandmother spoke up and stated, "We need two." She then began naming off who she felt should ride in it. In her sarcastic yet serious tone, Ashley said, "Are you paying for it?" There was no response. Ashley then said, "One car is sufficient." My only son's paternal grandmother felt she should have her own personal car. Why was I surprised? This was a home-going celebration for my only son. This was not about her wishes or demands. This was about burying my only son, whom I spent eighteen years raising without her. We made a decision, and it was behind us. Well, at least I thought it was behind us.

When we got home, I wanted to take a moment to catch my breath before we had visitors. There was a knock at the door. It was a church member, a lifelong friend of Willie's paternal grandmother, who had wasted no time to intercede on her behalf. She did not ask how we were, nor did she extend her condolences. The only thing out of her mouth was, "They need another car." I could not believe her nerve. My son was dead! She had the audacity to come declare what somebody else wanted.

Thank God we were not alone. Tommie, a family friend, was there. She said she would not have believed it if she did not see it for herself. The church member was unyielding. Eventually, Tommie escorted her to the door. I said nothing. I had washed my hands of the situation and would not revisit it under any circumstance. I made a conscious decision to give it to God.

CHAPTER 19

*Faith is taking the first step even when you don't see
the whole staircase.
~ Martin Luther King, Jr.*

*Wherefore I desire that ye faint not at my tribulations
for you, which is your glory. ~ Ephesians 3:13
King James Version (KJV)*

Chapter 19

I had many tests after Willie's death, especially the test of my faith. God was setting me up to experience His faithfulness, His love, and His grace. I would soon know I could trust Him through everything. God did not test me to bring me down, but to build me up. His will is for my good and His glory.

Following God's plan is not always easy, but I learned to trust that the all-knowing God will provide, lead, and strengthen me in my battles. Even in my suffering, I am victorious. No matter what situations, obstacles, or enemies I face, I can be confident, because Christ already won the greatest victory. He died on the cross for me. I believe God prepared me in His way, and when I pay attention to the signs, I know. Tomorrow is not promised to any of us. No one is exempt from death.

It was a day the Lord had made. I was determined to rejoice and be glad in it. God blessed us with a beautiful day of sunshine. I was determined to rejoice regardless of the circumstances. That was my attitude the morning of the funeral. The girls and I wore red and black, Willie's favorite colors. I had been blessed with a gift from Sandy Ellis, who gave me a beautiful black suit trimmed in gold and red. It was a perfect gift. We were dressed and ready to drive over to Bobby's, where everyone was to meet. The week had come full circle.

The girls and I prayed and headed over to Bobby's, only five minutes away. Slowly everyone arrived, except Willie's dad. We waited a little longer for him, but he was a "no show." Unbelievable! I shook my head, but I did not allow his absence to distract me. I could only think that, had his mother been concentrating on her son instead of spending energy and time sending a messenger to demand a family car, maybe he would be there.

The immediate family loaded up in our designated cars. It was a long, quiet ride. Willie's paternal grandmother attempted to make conversation, but I did not have words for her. Well, not any words she wanted to hear. This day could not end soon enough, so she could go back to doing what she did so well, ignoring my children, her grandchildren.

This was really happening. I was burying my

beloved son. No longer was I in denial; reality had set in. We arrived at the church, and there were literally thousands of people. I was taken aback. It was confirmation of what had been said all week, that Willie touched a lot of lives. I was grateful for the church allowing the services to be held there. Our home church would not have been able to accommodate the masses. There were just as many people outside as there were inside, but unlike those funerals of suburban students, which were broadcast on the six o'clock news, Willie's funeral was not mentioned. I remember thinking of Ice Cube's line in the movie *Boyz in the Hood* about watching the news after his brother had been shot down: "Either they don't know, don't show, or don't care."

As we slowly drove up to the curbside, I saw my beautician, Sherrie Jordan, a.k.a. Magnum Opus, leaving the church. Not long after, I saw Jay, Sherrie's sister, leaving the church too. They were unable to see me because of the tinted windows. People were literally walking over the hills and parking a good distance away. I found myself wondering, *did these people express how they felt to Willie while he was alive.*

I looked up and saw that my girlfriend Angeline had arrived. I was thankful she was present. We went way back. Lean, as I call her, had been around my kids when they were younger. I first met her at a doctor's office where I trained her as a medical assistant. We instantly became friends, and she dated my brother Darren. Lean was the kind of person who would give her last. She had come to see me through one of my most difficult days and to make certain the girls were well. This was not a surprise; it is who she is. I remember Willie's paternal grandmother asking who she was; Angeline was quick to address her concerns and any other questions she had.

It was not long before several vans from my place of employment arrived. I appreciated my employer for allowing my coworkers to support me. I thanked God for the lives Willie had touched and was grateful for the time God had allowed him to be with us.

We had been sitting in the car for a long time. I was feeling claustrophobic, sitting behind the driver, and I could not understand why we were still sitting in the car. I thought about how Willie probably felt the night of the accident, with his foot stuck in the door after the crash. He wanted out of that car. That is exactly how I felt, and I wanted out *now*.

As we entered the church, we were greeted by friends and family with hugs, kisses, and words of encouragement. We sat down front on the east side of the church. I had the end seat, which I preferred. Ashley was to my immediate right, then Michele, and then Angeline. My mom, brothers and sisters, and other immediate family members were seated behind me. At least, that is what I thought. Little did

I know that Willie's paternal grandmother had rearranged seating according to her personal preference.

She continued to be "on stage," and I'm not sure who she was trying to impress. Those that knew Willie had no idea who she was. It was obvious she wanted people to believe she was a wonderful grandmother. My brother, Darren, left his seat to view Willie's and Darshaun's bodies, and when he returned to his seat, a male friend of Willie's paternal grandmother was sitting in it. She had invited others to sit in the seats assigned to my mother and maternal grandmother. She had taken over the front row. Thank God this was kept from me the day of the service, or I may have done something I would possibly regret. I lost so much more respect for her. Her shenanigans continued throughout the service as well as the day.

Before the service officially got started, Willie's father arrived, reeking of alcohol. But I was unaware of this at the time too. I was not sitting close to him, but Michele even left for a moment to get away from the stench.

Willie's body was just a shell of who he used to be. Willie did not resemble Willie, but nevertheless it was the body of my beloved son. A picture of him in his William Jewel 87 jersey was in the program. After his Aunt Jackie's funeral Willie mentioned how he wanted his football picture to be included in the program. It was another small sign along the way. I had his jersey, the seven tickets, his picture, and a patch in the shape of a football with the number 87 engraved on it mounted in a large frame.

There were good-byes along the way. I believe that God prepares us. The question is whether we are paying attention to the signs given. The last week of high school, Willie had presented seven friends with a flower and a love note.

As I sat in the sanctuary waiting for the service to begin, I looked up and saw my boys, Terrence, William White, Matt Salary, Dancer, and several other track members, sitting together to my left in sort of a balcony area. Mike had arrived later. There was a rift between the boys after the accident, but they managed to remain respectful and sat together.

CHAPTER 20

When I stand before God at the end of my life, I would hope that I would not have a single bit of talent left, and could say, 'I used everything you gave me'.
~ Erma Bombeck

All the earth shall worship thee, and shall sing unto thee; they shall sing to thy name. Selah. ~ Psalm 66:4 King James Version (KJV)

Chapter 20

Time passed as I sat in anticipation of the service. Ashley kept an eye on what was going on around us. If she believed I was not attentive to her, she tapped my shoulder to get my attention. She also gave me play by play of those in attendance. She kept me posted on what was taking place.

When she saw Tanisha needing assistance down the aisle to view Willie, she nudged me. Tanisha was on the program to sing. Lynne Gordon, the vice principal of Hickman Mills, led her to the microphone and took the opportunity to share her thoughts of Willie and how he had influenced her. Tanisha sang "Hero" like I'd never heard her sing before. I still get emotional when I hear that song. Her voice rang through the sanctuary with power and anointing. Willie would have been pleased.

I also had requested that Kim Davis, sing. I am not certain she wanted to do it, but she was willing to do it for Willie. I have always enjoyed listening to Kim; she is one of those singers that doesn't do a lot of hand gestures but sings as well as, if not better than, those that are animated. Kim has a small frame, a beautiful cocoa-butter complexion, and a beautiful smile, and when she sings. The words flow effortlessly across her lips.

I had asked that Kim sing "The Battle Is the Lord's" by Yolanda Adams, and that day she owned it. Each note was melodic, and as she came to the end, even she was touched by the glory that reigned in the room. She stood at the microphone for a minute in celebration. I found myself on my feet, praising and thanking God for His goodness. Kim has always been able to reach deep into a soul and "sang," as the church folk would say. Willie was no longer with us, but I could only smile and know that his life was not in vain.

Our lives are never in vain when we do what Christ bids us to do. Our most mundane work leaves heavenly results. No labor is in vain that is produced in the Lord. Our ordinary work, in church, on our jobs, in the midst of life's worthlessness is transformed into joyful service. And like angel ministry, it leaves glorious results behind. The simplest things we do at Christ's bidding may become everlasting blessing to other souls or to our own.

The celebration of songs was glorious. But the highlight that day came in what Tyson said. He slowly moved toward the podium. He looked completely different from the young man I had met outside my home in tears and regret. He stood tall and confident, and he spoke very specifically about Willie's character. He shared his experience of Willie on the football field and the talent he displayed during football camp. He spoke as if he had known Willie all his life. He spoke of Willie's respectfulness, his sense of humor, his intelligence, and how he flirted with the girls.

Tyson shared how there was a young student who had come to dinner alone, and instead of allowing the student to eat alone, Willie opted to sit with him instead of with the football team. That was Willie. He was very giving of his time and himself. He was always willing to be the sacrifice.

Then Tyson shared the name that had been given to Willie at football camp: Whisper. He was *my* whisper from God that taught me contentment and how to trust. *My whisper from God! Whisper* summed up my son.

I was so proud Tyson was willing to speak at the service, being as soft-spoken as he was. He did an outstanding job.

As the service continued, one of the employees from

the major league team I work for brought me water. She kneeled on the floor and stayed there for the remainder of the service. She was an usher on the top level of the stadium. I thought it special that she was not ashamed to get a cup of water and bring it to me. And I'm not sure if she knew my son. But she knew me and cared enough to extend not only her condolences but to extend me a drink of water. At that moment she reminded me of an Old Testament servant. There was so many times Bible stories came to mind as that week played out.

Pastor William Kelly delivered Willie's eulogy. We had our disagreements, but he gave me some encouraging words several days prior to the service. He had not known Willie that long, but it did not take long to know Willie's character. He presented a memorable eulogy, and I am thankful for the Word brought forth.

Derald Conway, a high school classmate of mine, sang "Walk around Heaven" with his mom, Genetter Bradley, who was one of Darshaun's relatives. Darren was very moved by the selection of song, and I believe it encouraged his soul. This meant a lot to me. My brother, a barber by trade, worked in a shop right off Bannister and somehow he was unaware of the accident until the next day. Thank God he did not arrive at the shop that day, which would have been a traumatizing moment.

The service was beautiful. I praised God for bringing

so many people together. I was told that the following Sunday at Friendship Baptist Church the altar call was huge. All praises to God!

Before the close of the service, a last viewing was offered. Several athletes came and placed their medals on Willie's chest. It is such a sacrifice to have won a medal that meant so much only to never see it again by placing it inside a casket on a friend, teammate, competitor, and leader that would be placed in the ground. I thought of how, when we get to heaven, we will receive crowns but turn around and throw them at the feet of Jesus.

The attendants at the funeral home presented me with a key to his casket. I did not understand why. Why on earth would they give me a key to a casket that within the next half hour to an hour would be buried six feet under? Should I have his body exhumed? Would I find that the hospital removed my son's eyes and donated them without my consent? I still think about that today.

Willie's father did ride to the graveside with us. It was a quiet ride between us. The ride was so long. I remember looking back when the family car arrived at the intersection of Gregory Blvd and Highway 71, and the cars were still coming over the hill with bright headlights. As far as I could see, cars were still coming over the hills to the gravesite. I remember looking at my boys as they stood at the gravesite, having no desire to leave. Or maybe they wanted to leave but couldn't. I had really wanted them as pall bearers but did not think they would have been able to handle the request. They struggled with his death. Nevertheless, I should have given them the opportunity to say no.

Like most home-going ceremonies, the repast was held at my home church. After arriving at the church, as we were dealing with the plants, who was standing in my path yet again? You guessed it: Willie's paternal grandmother. She asked me if I had seen a plant that someone had told her was sent for her. No, I had not seen it, and I was sick of looking at her. What had disturbed me so much with her was that she had lost a child many years prior to my association with the family. I had always been told that when we go through something, we do not go through it for ourselves. We go through it so we can help the next person with what we learned. Maybe she had not learned anything from her experience. I am almost certain there had been others who said extreme things when I was not around, but she was unable to guard her tongue from Willie's death to his burial. I never received one kind or encouraging word from her.

The day finally came to a close. The plants and floral arrangements were put away and in the cars. My grandmother, mother, and other family members were holding on and keeping their cool. We entered the basement of the church, and it was filled with people. My church family had prepared a repast for the families. I was greeted by church members and was looking around to find a seat. However, when I opened the door to the library, I saw the room was full. There was no room for me and my daughters, and no one attempted to make room. I slowly closed the door and decided we would go home.

CHAPTER 21

*In the end, it's not the years in your life that count. It's
the life in your years. ~ Abraham Lincoln*

*Trust in the LORD with all your heart; do not depend
on your own understanding. ~ Proverbs 3:5
New Living Translation (NLT)*

Chapter 21

The world does not stop when tragedy happens. No one can stop time or turn back its hands. So prior to the accident, Willie, Michele, Ashley, and I had planned to see the new Denzel Washington movie, *Remember the Titans,* on Friday, September 29, 2000. It was about a football team previously coached by a white coach. A Black man (Denzel) began to coach the team, which would be a mixture of Black players and White players. The movie portrayed the struggles that arise from racial diversity.

With the funeral ironically being on the same date as the movie release, we decided to attend it the next day. All through the movie the number 87 stood out, as it always did. Regardless of what team is playing, 87 is one of my many triggers.

My daughters and some close family friends

attended the showing. No one had any idea about the car accident in the movie prior to attending. So you can only imagine the reaction to the scene when one of the prominent players was a victim of a car accident. We all sat there in the theater holding our breath. They were looking at me, and I was looking straight ahead. The accident was not fatal for the football player. However, he would later die in the movie. Talk about reliving a moment. It was even more ironic that Ashley would graduate and attend Spelman College the next year, where she met and got the autograph of Herman Boone, the coach played by Denzel.

In the days to come the hardest things were the simple ones. The things that used to be so routine like going to the grocery store became a chore. I had decided not to go to the grocery store until one day Michele said, "Momma, we still have to eat." She was right, but everything reminded me of Willie, including and especially food.

I remember my first Sunday back at church after his death. It was the part in the service when we stood to sing a congregational hymn. Midway through the song, I stopped singing. I could not sing it with the conviction I once knew. As my eyes filled with tears, I excused myself from the sanctuary to go where I could allow my tears to flow freely. But it was not long before the bathroom was filled with women desiring to console me.

Yes, I was sad. Behind every smile was a tear, but I had to remember that God would see me through each and every problem I encountered. Problems are a constant in life. That will never change. What changed was my power to deal with those problems. God allowed tribulation to come into my life not to hurt me, but to teach me to lean on Him. He taught me how to trust Him.

Out-of-ordinary situations that come into my life bring different emotions: sorrow, gloom, distress, happiness, and so on, which were normal reactions to my good and bad encounters. But how long will it take for my heart and my faith to kick in? How long will it take for me to say, "I trust in His will, and I can rejoice no matter what the Lord brings my way"?

Even when all seems dark and when everything seems to be falling apart, He still is a God who wants the best for my life. Even my sad and tragic events were molded into something positive. God's promise made to me, through Christ's love on the cross, declares that this situation will not overpower God's presence within me and alongside me. God is so great. God is so loving that He is making it all work for my good.

CHAPTER 22

We must be willing to let go of the life we have planned,
so as to have the life that is waiting for us
~ E. M. Forster

For I know the plans I have for you," says the LORD.
"They are plans for good and not for disaster, to give
you a future and a hope. ~ Jeremiah 29:11
New Living Translation (NLT)

Chapter 22

Slowly, I began to trust God's plan. I walked by faith. I couldn't see the final outcome, but God knew. If I knew, there would be no need for faith. I know from my own experience how God guided me through times of trouble to an unexpected outcome. Not being able to see the ending, I simply had to trust. Sometimes you just have to hang on, believing God is working things out for good, which He will.

God always gives His people victory. And He has used me, one of His least likely people. None of us experience victory with a weak, hopeless faith. God's plans make no sense to me, but courageous faith that kept me going when I made my unforeseen journey through the valley has seen me through. God does not provide a full picture of His plans, because He knows it may overwhelm us. But that is the point. There is no way I could fulfill the mission He had for me without Him empowering me.

Immediately after the accident, I was confronted with the fact that Willie was gone, and if I heard it once I heard it a thousand times, "Time will heal." Whose time? Was it a time measured by a clock or a time in which my personal life would move forward? I saw healing in neither.

God reminded me of Jeremiah 29:11: He knows what He is doing and He has it all planned out to take care of me and not abandon me. Plans to give me the future I hope for. I could hear God saying, "I have a purpose—not for you personally, but for the glory of God." Yet in the moment I could not see His purpose. The plan was custom designed for me and me alone—not to mention the plan God had for Willie. But He chose to use him in a way that was far greater than anything Willie or any of us who knew him could have imagined. My question to God was not "Why?" but "Why now?" I thank God for my friend Christi, who reminded me of God's sovereignty.

We have been assigned to run the race that God has set for us—not the race we set for ourselves or the race that other people set for us. If you try to run any other race, you will be unsuccessful; you will often find yourself tired and frustrated.

God's plan for your future is found in His Word, not in the latest magazines or in a how-to book. You cannot find the plans for your life if you are looking in the wrong places.

CHAPTER 23

The best way out is always through.
~ Robert Frost

For everything there is a season, a time for every
activity under heaven. ~ Ecclesiastes 3:1
New Living Translation (NLT)

Chapter 23

There is a time for everything. And I found that escaping from reality was my mini retreat. In the process of escaping, I found myself in compromising locations. There was one night, and one night only. That was all it took. I had driven to the cemetery by myself. This had not been a planned trip. I had left the house to get a change of scenery and found myself in the neighborhood of Forest Hills Cemetery. The sun had set.

I was scared of the cemetery during the day. I could hear my grandmother's voice telling me there was no need to be scared of those that were dead; it was the living that should concern me. I laughed at myself as I continued to drive toward the cemetery. What had come over me? I turned into the entrance gate and slowly drove to Willie's gravesite. With little hesitation, I pulled off the road, put the car in park, and got out. Crazy, right? You would think by this time I would have come to my senses and fled, but I was determined to go; I think I was expecting some answer from God.

I walked slowly across the grass until I arrived at his headstone. I looked around scared that any minute something would send me running out of there without the car. Astonished, at myself, I had to ask myself what I was doing. Had I completely lost my mind? Anything could have happened to me. It was one of those instances when you ask yourself, "How did I get here?" I had broken my own cardinal rule: never travel alone and always let someone know where you are.

There I stood in the cemetery after dark for no reason. I had no agenda. I found myself standing in the dark in the middle of a closed cemetery attempting to run away from the inevitable: life. Once I got back in the car, I did a little crying, a little praying, and left.

I thought I knew the height and depth of God's love for me until Willie died. I would often feel as if God was not there. I admit there were times I would cry, asking, "God, where are you? Why am I going through this?" He was there. He is a God that cannot lie. When He says He will never leave or forsake you that is what He means.

He was there all the time. It was His amazing,

sufficient grace that had kept me through the accident and every day that followed. God could have accomplished whatever He was doing in my life in a number of ways, but this was the journey assigned to me, and I had to trust Him. Willie was gone. I could not change that fact. My desperate need to escape would be just that—a desperate need to run away.

That was not the only place I ran away to. The other place was the casino. I did not and still do not care to drive. However, the casino was twenty miles one way, a thirty-minute drive. I do not like being out late at night, which was a red flag that my second choice of flight was not a good thing. That's why it's called an "escape from reality." I was running away from the truth. The truth was that Willie was dead, and no matter what I ran to, he was not coming back.

I tried to escape reality because there was a void and I had no idea what would now be in his place. I am a creature of habit, and I liked the routine I had with Willie when I called him, when I saw him. But my routine was no longer needed, because Willie was gone. My escape was a void that I was filling with bad habits.

Willie had been something good in my life. Why on earth was I willing to replace something good with something bad? I was afraid. I was afraid of the unknown and what my life would be without him. I could not see past his death. But God! God made it clear that the habits I found comforting would begin to control my life.

I had been operating on autopilot. Memories of Willie were triggers. Now when triggers presented themselves, I began to replace the habits with prayer and reading the Word. The habits did not disappear overnight. It was not easy, but I never gave up, which was the answer to my victory. Not giving up! God needed me to be still. I often grew anxious and would get in a hurry. I wanted things to happen in a rush. I did not understand my breakthrough was in His plan. But I needed to be still and know. Be still and know.

Rachelle Law

CHAPTER 24

"Still I Rise"
~ Maya Angelou

I took another walk around the neighborhood and realized that on this earth as it is —
The race is not always to the swift,
Nor the battle to the strong,
Nor satisfaction to the wise,
Nor riches to the smart,
Nor grace to the learned.
Sooner or later bad luck hits us all.
~ Ecclesiastes 9:11
The Message (MSG)

Chapter 24

My first day back at work was Monday, October 2, 2000. A copy of the devotional guide *Our Daily Bread* was just as I'd left it, lying flat on my desk, resting in front of the telephone, opened to the reading for September 21, 2000. Mike Levy, my boss at the time, was vice president of marketing. He longed to ask me something but was hesitant. He walked over to my desk and pointed out this sentence: "A strong, healthy man drops dead. A rising young athlete contracts a crippling disease. A person of means suddenly loses everything in a bad deal." This resonated something in him, as it did within me the first time I read it, which had been over a week before. Could it be this was how I was able to keep my composure the night of the accident? Because of the Word that had been planted in my spirit? I do remember it struck a chord in me; maybe that is what the Bible means when it talks about a familiar spirit or a cloud of witnesses — something like that.

It's Not over Till It's Over

The newspaper headline read, "Jockey Beats Horse over Finish Line." The jockey beat the pack by 20 lengths and his horse by one length when he was catapulted out of the saddle and over the finish line. His horse, which had tripped, followed soon after. But the victory went to the second-place finisher named Slip Up. A race official said that the jockey "was so far in front that only a freak accident would stop him, and that's what happened.

We've all experienced life's unexpected happenings. The author of Ecclesiastes took note of them when he said, "The race is not to the swift, nor the battle to the strong" (9:11). He reflected on the fact that man is not the master of his destiny, as he so often thinks he is.

Life is filled with unpredictable experiences and events. They seem like stones dropped into the gears of human ingenuity. A strong, healthy man drops dead. A rising young athlete contracts a crippling disease. A person of means suddenly loses everything in a bad deal.

What can we learn from this? Not to trust our own strength, our own wisdom, or our own skill, but to depend on the Lord who alone knows the end from the beginning.

Life's race is not over till He says it's over.
There's so much now I cannot see, my eyesight's far too dim; But come what may, I'll simply trust and leave it all to Him. --Overton
Living without faith in God is like driving in the fog.

Ecclesiastes 9:11 – 911, the number called in emergencies. That was one of the first things I yelled after the accident: "Someone please call 911." Michele had beamed when she shared how they sang "911" all the way home en route to the homecoming events. I look at God and how He orchestrated the time allowed for Willie to spend with each of his sister's one on one. I enjoyed that song until the accident; it became hard to hear after his death.

For me, returning to work was a welcome change. Work was the only part of my life that seemed to be a normal routine. Many coworkers continued to share how sorry they were. I said thank you and kept it moving. I was able to concentrate because I believed the people I worked with sincerely cared. I did not fear breaking down in front them.

Plenty of pictures graced my desk. I did not rearrange the photographs of Willie nor did I put them away. I welcomed his presence. I do not know if it bothered my coworkers; if it did, they never told me. Healing from the death of a loved one is a slow process, and getting back to work was an important step in my journey.

There was no set order for the flow of sadness, anger, and acceptance that came over me. Every emotion was justifiable. I found myself reliving the accident continuously and wishing it was all a dream. I struggled when I met new people and they asked how many children I had. I would never see this person again, and it was not worth explaining that Willie, my only son, was dead. And yet when I said I had two children to avoid that problem, I felt terrible, as if I had betrayed him.

Yes, life does go on. When the fiery trials come in your life, and they will come, focus on Jesus. He is your very BFF (best friend forever) and knows exactly how to bring you through each and every trial. Do not allow your circumstances to dictate the issues in your life or to drag you down. Look up! Focus on *Jesus*! He's standing there with outstretched arms, waiting to receive you, comfort you, and show you the way through to better things ahead. Time may not cause us to forget, but it does provide some space for healing.

Each day brought its own challenges. There were the notorious milestones after the loss of a loved one. The first event we faced was the night of the Ashley's cotillion.

She wore a beautiful white gown and satin gloves as she stood in a receiving line full of beautiful young woman and was introduced to the audience. Typically, a debutante is presented by her father, but Willie had been scheduled to do the honor. Once again she would be in the limelight and once again she would be standing alone because of the accident. That was a bit unsettling. But she pressed on and had the support of the school, family, and the church.

Uncle Bobby did the honor of escorting and presenting her in the absence of her brother at the ball. It was fitting that the song selected for the dance was "Still I Rise" by Yolanda Adams. Ashley had overcome many overwhelming circumstances, and her big brother would have been very proud of her.

After Willie's death, I was confronted with some of the things that would never happen. I never thought attending a wedding would be a trigger until it was too late. I was already sitting in the pew in the church at a family wedding. I had looked forward to the wedding and festivities, but shortly after I was escorted to my seat by the usher, an overwhelming flood of emotions overcame me. I began to cry, not for the bride or the groom, but because of the thought of never seeing Willie marry. The more I tried to suppress the tears, the more uncontrollable they became. I began to think of the wedding Willie would never have and the grandchildren that would never exist. The moment was unbearable.

Rachelle Law

CHAPTER 25

Life isn't a matter of milestones, but of moments.
~ Rose Kennedy

He hath made every thing beautiful in his time: also he hath set the world in their heart, so that no man can find out the work that God maketh from the beginning to the end. ~ Ecclesiastes 3:11
King James Version (KJV)

Chapter 25

Christmas traditions have changed in my family over the years. Many have changed because Grandma Mary is no longer with us. But my girls and I decided to start our first season without Willie by inviting friends and family to join us in putting up the Christmas tree on his birthday, December 1. We took this time to celebrate with music, food, and fun. For the creative piece of the evening, we held a gingerbread house decorating competition. And we have carried on this tradition. Those in attendance change from year to year, but it is always a good time.

Christmas was Willie's favorite holiday. He loved everything that surrounded the day. Be it the celebration of the birth of Christ or the gift-giving side of it, he loved it all.

December is one of the hardest months for me. Willie and Darshaun shared the same birth date along with Kevin Monroe and Mary Williams, Willie's children's director at church, who was very dear and special to Willie. They called each other "birthday buddies."

Christmas is the one holiday when the entire family came together. Given that Grandma Mary was no longer with us, we took turns hosting Christmas. This was the first family outing I would attend since the funeral. It was being held at Darren's townhouse. There was plenty of room for everybody. The kids had a place where they could be kids, and there was plenty of room for unexpected but welcome guests who may stop by.

I sat quietly with the family, staring off into the distance with glassy eyes. My thoughts were as far away as the sunset. I could not hide my sadness behind a fake smile. I am sure they could see the pain in my eyes. There were two bathrooms: one on the main floor and the other on the second. I decided to go to the upstairs bathroom, hoping I would not be missed.

I was wrong. The door was slightly ajar, and as I reach for a Kleenex to blot my tears, I could hear the eerie creaking of the hinges. It was Ashley peeking in. She pushed the door open, inviting herself in. She asked if I was crying, and though my back was to her, I could not tell a lie. She said, "Go ahead and cry, Momma." As if I needed her permission. I laughed just at the thought of her comment. I sniffled a little, wiped my face, and refreshed my makeup. Ashley grabbed my hand as if she was my mother, and we returned to the family gaiety downstairs.

As I went down the stairs, I could hear my brother having words with my mom. She had been probing behind the Christmas tree. Darren seemed to be irritated, as he sternly recommended my mom stay away from the Christmas tree. She went right on being inquisitive as if he'd said nothing at all. He had placed his camera on a tripod to capture the holiday memories. We had lost several family members in a short time and wanted to capture the moments of the day.

Not too long after I sat down, I heard my mom say, "Uh oh," as she fell behind the Christmas tree. I am ashamed to say the sight of my mom falling as if in slow motion caused me to go into unstoppable, hysterical laughter. I could not stop, not even to make sure she was okay. As sad as my behavior was, unfortunately, no one helped her. It was a Kodak moment. No one could resist getting a picture of the episode.

I could not contain my laughter as I watched my mother lying under the Christmas tree. And there was no mercy extended by family. As she slowly got her bearings and got up, it was paparazzi frenzy, cameras flashing everywhere. I began to scream a high-pitched scream.

I know you are probably shaking your head in disappointment in our behavior. What kind of family watches a family member fall and no one lends a hand? Yours, probably. LOL.

Have you ever laughed so hard you couldn't breathe? I could not catch my breath. I was bent over holding my side, which was cramping. The pitch of my laughter became higher and higher. As crazy and awkward as it was, this was the first time I had genuinely laughed since the accident.

Rachelle Law

CHAPTER 26

"A thief believes everybody steals."
~ Edgar Watson Howe

The thief cometh not, but for to steal, and to kill, and to destroy: I am come that they might have life, and that they might have it more abundantly. ~ John 10:10 King James Version (KJV)

Chapter 26

Some have encounters and forget them; they become lost in routine again, losing the awareness or and the wonder of the encounter. It is my understanding that when there is an encounter with the divine, there are three things: deep transformation, deep insight, and great inspiration. A few months after Christmas, I had a spiritual encounter that transformed my life.

It was close to 3:00 a.m. on April 7, 2001. I was unable to sleep. I had been thinking of Willie, reflecting on the loss. I began to whisper prayers and praises to God, crying. When I glanced at the clock again, it showed 5:30 a.m.

I was certain I could sleep then. As I arranged my pillows and decided to close my eyes, a spirit entered the room. No, I was not asleep; therefore, I was not dreaming. I was wide awake and lying in the bed, and not only could I see the spirit, I also could feel its presence. It was a dark shadow that slowly moved from the base of the wall and then up the wall and across the ceiling.

As I lay there, I was not afraid, but in disbelief. I'd heard of such experiences, but this was my first. The smoldering, black cloud covered the walls and began to come upon me. It was directly above me before descending on me. I could feel it as it filled my chest cavity and slowly moved down until it reached the pit of my stomach. Once it positioned itself in my stomach region, it shook my insides — literally. It was as if something was being deposited, but it was not of God. The closest thing I can compare it to was in a scene in the movie *Ghost*, when silhouettes moved through the streets after someone died.

I got out of bed and quickly left my bedroom, calling my daughters in the next room. Snot was running from my nose full blast, like a running faucet. It was unbelievable. Unless you have experienced something like this, you may find it hard to believe. Like Thomas, you would have to see it to believe it. Not knowing and completely understanding what was going on, I felt led to talk with some of my spiritual leaders.

In my Christian journey I have been fortunate to have many MWOG (Mighty Women of God) in my life who has contributed to my spiritual growth. These women have been deliberately placed in my life. Rev. Janet Johnson, Mrs. Margaret Byers, Mrs. Hazel Byers, and Christi Evans are but a few I called that morning. I was not sure if it was a visit from God or from the enemy. The more I thought about it, the more I was convinced because of the darkness that it was the enemy. I was not sure what was going to happen next. At that point I wanted some answers. It was as if something was being deposited in my spirit.

I was unable to reach Christi and Mrs. Hazel. I had been praying and seeking God, so I knew God was with me regardless of what was going on, so I was not afraid. Some people had similar experiences of such encounters and were sure beyond a shadow of a doubt that it was definitely a visit from the enemy and that his plan was to destroy me. The enemy will always press in hardest when he has the most at stake—the most to lose. He wanted me to die in the loss of my son. I was under a spiritual attack designed to take me out.

God has placed greatness in all of us. And no devil in hell is going to take that away. So what do you do when you are under spiritual attack? Know that defeat is not an option for kingdom people. God has given us spiritual authority to cast down, bind, and loose the enemy. One thing I know for sure is that even in the wee hours of the morning there are women I am able to call on. I can only encourage you to surround yourself with people who are going to lift you higher. Surround yourself with good people on purpose. Arleatha Green, a spiritual mother, encouraged me and reminded me to take the authority I have been given and confront the evil spirit before it killed me.

Rachelle Law

CHAPTER 27

*In three words I can sum up everything I've learned
about life: it goes on.*
~ Robert Frost

*Yet in all these things we are more than conquerors
through Him who loved us. ~ Romans 8:37
New King James Version (NKJV)*

Chapter 27

It had been a difficult journey. I had returned to work, resumed responsibilities at church, and had overcome many milestones, but I was still hurting and I was tired of hurting. Then Christi sent me an e-mail. She is the friend who always held me accountable. We had begun to spend more time together walking and did an evening Bible study in addition to my Wednesday-night Bible study at church. Attending Bible study with Christi was one of the best decisions I made during my grieving season.

The subject line of the e-mail she sent me read, "Are you in pain?" *Are you serious?* Then I considered the source from which it came. I opened the e-mail and began to read it. Although I was at work, you would have never known it. Being at work did not stop me from allowing myself to surrender to the emotions I was feeling. The e-mail referred to the book of Job, beginning with the thirty-eighth chapter. As I read, I began to cry. My work station was in a high-traffic area, but I was not interrupted while I read that day.

"Where were you when I laid the foundation" was the first line that sent chills all over my body. I did not feel I was questioning God about why Willie died; I was questioning His timing. But did it make any difference? Who did I think I was? Well, this was the day that I was reminded of who I was and from where I had come. I am nothing but dust, and had it not been for the breath of life given by God, I would not be here, nor would Willie.

Everything was laid before me. What were my credentials? Who did I think I was? Had I ever created anything? Had I given life to anything? I carried Willie and birthed him, but I had not given him life. Did I have control of the air and the sea? God smacked me in my face and reminded me that I thought I was all that. I thought I knew everything. I thought I had all the answers.

My face was wet with my tears and never once while reading did I stop to wipe either my face or my nasty nose. I kept right on reading and hearing just what the Lord wanted to say to me. As I sat there reading and purging, I felt a burden lift.

It was as if I was on trial in a courtroom. One question came after another, and all I could do was listen and receive: Do you? Can you? Where were you? When did you? Who has? Who can? Nothing was left uncovered; not an animal, not a situation, not a circumstance.

Why was this hitting me so hard? Because the Word reminded me of whom I am and who I belonged to. The Word reminded me that I was not sovereign, I was not in control, and I needed to stop tripping. Yes, stop tripping! God had given me a son. God did that! God allowed me to raise Him. God did that! God provided. God healed. God delivered.

God had given him to me for a season, and I was grateful and had found myself feeling as if I was sovereign and I knew best. I sat there and asked myself, *who do I think I am?* It was not that God did not understand, because He did. Nor was it that He did not care, because He did. In that moment I was reminded when I stood at the accident scene and said, "If this cup could pass, not my will, Lord, but Your will be done." I surrendered, and God's will was done. It was the expected end. I continued to cry as tears ran down my face.

I could barely see the words in front of me, but I continued to read the book of Job. It is a wonder I did not cry my contacts right out of my eyes. My face was soaking wet. I did not care that black lines of makeup streaked my face. I did not care that I had the ugly cry going on at work. God had reminded me that I am not exempt and all things would work together.

Not until that day was I able to let go. I did not "forsake the assembly" by not attending church, but I was merely going through the motions as I had been doing with everything else in my life. Life goes on, with or without you.

The loss taught me a lot about myself, about life, and about seizing the moments with friends and family. We get one chance at life, and if we are like Willie, we live it to the fullest and touch somebody along the way. I am forever grateful for someone who touched me along the way. Thanks, Christi. Job is where I go when I need to be reminded of who I am in God's eyes.

☙

Rachelle Law

CHAPTER 28

The best and most beautiful things in the world cannot be seen or even touched - they must be felt with the heart.
~ Helen Keller

Owe no one anything except to love one another, for he who loves another has fulfilled the law. ~ Romans 13:8 New King James Version (NKJV)

Chapter 28

There continued to be different ways organizations and individuals chose to recognize and honor Willie. The following track season. The 2001 Hickman Mills track team recognized Willie, by wearing an emblem of a pair of track shoes with wings on their track uniforms. There were several different scholarships given in his name.

I could not grasp the half of what God intended for Willie. God continued to bless his legacy years after he was gone. One in particular comes to mind. Eric Frizell was a young man that had attended Ruskin High School, the school Darshaun attended. Eric did not know Willie personally, yet he was inspired by all Willie accomplished and how he had managed to maintain both academic and athletic success.

Eric was very thoughtful through the grieving

process. He never forgot us on the special anniversary dates. For Christmas he baked the best cookies. Eric also set out to have a memorial at the high school. Eric thought Willie, a.k.a. Clarence W. Smith Jr., was the model student-athlete at Hickman. So he had set out to share with current and future students how Willie had great success in the classroom, on the football field, and on the track.

After Eric pulled a rabbit out of a hat, he managed to have a plaque mounted on the track field where Willie spent many countless hours training for his state medal in 2000.

The plaque was unveiled on May 24, 2009. In attendance were former teachers, coaches, teammates, classmates, friends and family. An unexpected presentation was made from Jamal, who had run in a relay in the state competition the following year, in which the relay team took first. He gave me the baton that they had carried in the race. I felt so blessed for all the love shown in recognition of Willie that day.

The ceremony was closed with a four-hundred-meter dedication, and, yes, I did participate in the run. The high school has been transformed into a middle school, but the plaque remains on the east wall of the track. A picture still decks the hall outside the gymnasium in recognition of his state meet title. Words are not enough to describe the effort, time, and hard work that went into making the dedication come to fruition. Like the baton Jamal presented to me, I wrote this book as the baton to be passed on in the relay of life.

I've had many ups and downs since the accident. I founded an organization to address the issues of domestic violence. I held my first workshop, "How Come, How long," in 2004.

My mom was diagnosed with cancer in 2009. The next year she married a lifelong friend who she had known since she was ten. Mr. Gilbert was a blessing to my mom and our family. I have since remarried too.

My daughters have been successful in their careers, despite the fact that the loss of their brother was very difficult. Ashley often would say she did not lose a part of herself, she lost half of herself. Michele misses his presence, especially when she celebrates new accomplishments.

I could say everything happens for a reason, or I could say you should make lemonade if life hands you a lemon. In life we have options when things happen. I have learned I can mope and complain, or I can say, "Why not me." I learned to glorify God at every opportunity. My journey is a mere glimpse of my life. I can now turn the negative into the positive and embrace what life throws my way. I could easily throw it back, but that would be giving up or surrendering. When something comes my way, I can now knock it out of the park.

There are times it seems the journey will never end. There continue to be road blocks, potholes, a few rest stops, and some transfer stations but for the most part it has been an adventure with curves that kept me holding on to God's hand. My journey has not ended, and who knows what tomorrow will bring, but now I know that same God that picked me for His team has kept me on His roster. Regardless of the strikeouts and the walks, He has never left me.

Willie did not have a loud voice. He didn't compete with the noisy environment. He was polite and usually spoke in a whisper rather than a shout. Yet he demanded your attention. If you didn't hear his soft whisper in his laugh, touch, presence, or smile, chances are you were not listening. His whispers changed lives. The subtle, gentle vibrations of his vocal cords were soft whispers from God. He was my gift, my whisper from God.

Willie and Darshaun

State Track Meet 2000

Willie and Ashley Homecoming

*"Me" and Willie's sisters: Michele and Ashley
(Photographer Quiera Young)*

Rachelle Law

Rachelle Law

Made in the USA
Charleston, SC
25 August 2013